SOUTHERN RAILWAY
Through PassengerService
In Color

GREG STOUT

Copyright © 2005
Morning Sun Books, Inc.
All rights reserved. This book may not be reproduced in part or in whole without written permission from the publisher, except in the case of brief quotations or reproductions of the cover for the purposes of review.

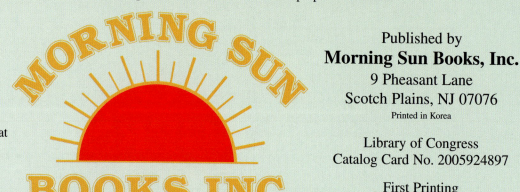

To access our full library *In Color* visit us at
www.morningsunbooks.com

Published by
Morning Sun Books, Inc.
9 Pheasant Lane
Scotch Plains, NJ 07076
Printed in Korea

Library of Congress
Catalog Card No. 2005924897

First Printing
ISBN 1-58248-166-0

ROBERT J. YANOSEY, President

DEDICATION
For Marilyn. We miss you, still.

ACKNOWLEDGMENTS

In any work of history such as this one, the end product is not the result of the efforts of one individual. Instead, the writer relies upon the generous assistance of many others, including historians, editors, proof-readers, photographers, librarians and amateur psychologists, who, when failure looms, talk the writer back off the ledge.

In this work I have been blessed twice over, first, by publisher Bob Yanosey, who entrusted the project to me in the first place, and second, by the many photographers who unselfishly exhibited a willingness to contribute their precious photos to bring this volume to life. Among those are Jim Thorington, of Birmingham, Alabama, whose work appears in many locations. Heartfelt thanks must also go to my good friend George Strombeck. Despite having worked with George on previous productions, I am still amazed at the depth and quality of his photography. Readers who have not previously seen George's photos will be blown away by what he has achieved in terms of visual history. Other old friends deserving of mention are Dr. Louis Marre of the University of Dayton, former Rock Island publicist Jim Neubauer and author/publisher Robert J. Wayner, all railroad historians of considerable note. In addition, I am grateful for the kind assistance of Rodger Darling, Paul Coe, Lyle Key and Gib Allbach, each of whom answered the bell without hesitation. In addition to the above, the works of many other photographers and collectors appear, including Emery Gulash, J. W. Swanberg, Lawson Hill, Paul Winters, Bernie Wooler, George Berisso, Matt Herson, Douglas Nuckles and Mac Owen, to name just a few. To all of you, and to those whose names I may have omitted, please accept my gratitude. Thanks also goes to the University of Missouri at St. Louis, caretaker of the John Barriger Collection of the St. Louis Mercantile Library. Within those four walls lies a treasure of information that cannot be duplicated in any other venue.

Finally, although more than a year of research and effort went into pulling this book together, I have no doubt that there exist errors of both fact and inference. To the extent that they do, the fault is entirely my own, and I can only hope that they do not greatly detract from the enjoyment of the finished work.

Greg Stout
Bartlett, Illinois
February 2005

BIBLIOGRAPHY

- Cheney, Fred D. and Sweetland, David R., *Southern Railway In Color*, Morning Sun Books, 1994
- Dubin, Arthur D., *Some Classic Trains*, Kalmbach Publishing Company, 1964
- Frailey, Fred, *Twilight of the Great Trains*, Kalmbach Publishing Company, 1998
- Holland, Kevin J., "The Frugal Approach," *Dream Trains*, Kalmbach Publishing Company, 2003
- Kinkaid, James, *Southern Railway Color Guide to Freight and Passenger Equipment*, Morning Sun Books, 1996.
- *Official Guide to the Railways*, various editions.
- Phillips, Don, "The Railroad That Stayed Out of Amtrak", *Trains*, Kalmbach Publishing Company, October 1974.
- Prince, Richard, *Southern Railway Steam Locomotives and Boats*, Richard Prince, 1970 (rev. ed.)
- Schafer, Mike, "Crescent Cousins", *Passenger Train Journal*, PTJ Publishing, Park Forest, IL, October/November 1980
- Schafer, Mike and Welsh, Joe, *Classic American Streamliners*, Motorbooks International, 1997
- Tillotson, Curt, Jr., *Southern Railway Diesel Locomotives and Trains*, TLC Publishing Inc., 2003.
- Warden, William E., *Norfolk & Western Passenger Service 1946-1971*, TLC Publishing, Inc., 1990
- Wayner, Robert, *Car Names and Consists*, Wayner Publications, 1972
- Withers, Paul K., *Diesels of the Southern Railway 1939-1982*, Withers Publishing, 1997

SOUTHERN RAILWAY THROUGH PASSENGER SERVICE In Color

1941-1960:
THE "SILVER TRAINS" 4

1960-1970:
DISILLUSIONMENT AND DECLINE 22

1971-1979:
GOING OUT IN STYLE 86

APPENDIX A: SOUTHERN RAILWAY
STREAMLINED PASSENGER CAR ROSTER 126

APPENDIX B: SOUTHERN RAILWAY
PASSENGER DIESEL POWER ROSTER 128

SOUTHERN RAILWAY
Through
PASSENGER SERVICE
In Color

For Southern Railway, the era of streamlined passenger trains arrived in the years immediately prior to the onset of World War II. First on the scene were four lightweight motor trains, a joint effort among Southern, Fairbanks-Morse and St. Louis Car Company. Next, in 1941, came the beautiful new streamlined SOUTHERNER and TENNESSEAN trains. The war years temporarily halted further expansion of the streamliner fleet, but the postwar period saw further growth by way of the NEW ROYAL PALM and the stainless steel version of the flagship CRESCENT.

Unlike many other railroads, Southern's passenger service did not expand a fleet, as with Rock Island's ROCKETS, Missouri Pacific's EAGLES or Santa Fe's CHIEFS. Instead, Southern reliably "Served the South" with Pullman green heavyweight trains that, save for the diesel power up front, would have looked right at home three or four decades earlier.

In the late 1950s, Southern's passenger business began to unravel, as the jet and the Interstate Highway lured passengers in increasing numbers away from the rails. Like most other carriers, Southern did its best, first to hang onto the business it had, and when that failed, to shed its remaining trains as quickly (and sometimes as ruthlessly) as possible. By the time the Federal government intervened in May 1971 with the creation of Amtrak, Southern was down to four pairs of passenger trains, including only two, the SOUTHERN CRESCENT and the PIEDMONT, that actually went anywhere.

And then a wondrous thing happened. For reasons having to do in equal measure with economics and corporate pride, Southern declined the Amtrak escape route and continued to operate its pared-down passenger business almost into the 1980s. As a part of that operation, it fielded what was widely acclaimed the best passenger train in the country, the Washington-New Orleans SOUTHERN CRESCENT. Alas, not all wonders are meant to last, and so it was with the CRESCENT. New management, rising costs and obsolete equipment brought the storybook service to an end in 1979.

In text and picture form, this volume tells the story of Southern's passenger trains, beginning in 1939 and concluding with the last run of the SOUTHERN CRESCENT in February 1979. It is divided into three chapters that cover the years 1940-1960, 1961-1970 and 1971-1979. Within those chapters, we will review the operations of some of Southern's best known trains, including the CRESCENT, ROYAL PALM, TENNESSEAN, PELICAN, BIRMINGHAM SPECIAL and KANSAS CITY-FLORIDA SPECIAL. We'll also take a brief look at competitors such as Seaboard and Louisville & Nashville, and neighboring roads like Frisco, Illinois Central and Central of Georgia. And while a complete history of SR passenger service is beyond the scope of this volume, both the publisher and I are confident that Southern fans, old and new, will enjoy being along for the ride. *Welcome Aboard. We're glad you could join us!*

SOUTHERN RAILWAY THROUGH PASSENGER SERVICE
1941-1960: THE "SILVER TRAINS"

Depending upon one's point of view, the era of streamlined trains arrived on the Southern Railway System either in 1939 or in 1941. In the earlier instance, at the beginning of 1939, Southern ordered six lightweight "motor trains" from St. Louis Car Company. Conceptually, the Southern motor trains were cast in much the same mold as the "doodlebug" gas-electric cars that had long been operating on various railroads throughout the Midwest and South since the late 1920s. They were short trains intended to run over short distances in daylight, offering limited amenities. Each of SR's new two-unit trains consisted of a Fairbanks-Morse diesel-powered rail car that incorporated a cab, an engine room, a baggage compartment and a railway post office (RPO) section. Trailing each power car was a single, 76-seat air-conditioned coach.

Variously christened the GOLDENROD, the JOE WHEELER, the VULCAN and the CRACKER (a name that would be unlikely to fly in today's politically correct America), the green-and-aluminum (*not* silver) trains made their public debuts at St. Louis Union Station. After a brief public display, the trains headed for home, each as Train No. 23, where they settled into their regular assignments on runs between Birmingham-Mobile, Alabama; Oakdale, Tennessee - Tuscumbia, Alabama; Atlanta - Brunswick, Georgia; and Meridian, Mississippi-Chattanooga, Tennessee respectively. As things turned out, the little trains were reasonably successful and continued in Southern service into the 1950s, when they were sold to short lines Georgia Northern and Georgia & Florida.

The *real* streamliners arrived in 1941. Faced with competition, especially from Louisville & Nashville, Seaboard Air Line and Atlantic Coast line, all of whom had upgraded their Florida trains, and pressured by the Atlanta *Journal*, which grumped in its editorial pages about the city's lack of streamlined passenger service, Southern took the plunge. With some misgivings, in October 1940, SR ordered 41 lightweight cars from Pullman-Standard. These were intended to equip two new trains: The Washington, DC-Memphis TENNESSEAN, and an all-coach streamliner, the SOUTHERNER, which entered service between New York and New Orleans on March 31, 1941.

The SOUTHERNER equipment order included three baggage-dormitory-coaches, three 52-seat divided ("Jim Crow") coaches, six 56-seat conventional coaches, three 48-seat dining cars and three tavern-lounge-observation cars. As part of the same lot, three more 56-seat coaches were purchased by the Pennsylvania Railroad, which provided through-car service for the SOUTHERNER between Washington and New York.

The order for TENNESSEAN equipment included four baggage-RPO cars in two different configurations, two baggage-mail cars, three Jim Crow coaches, nine 56-seat conventional coaches, two diners and three flat-ended tavern-observation cars. All the new equipment was finished in unpainted stainless steel with black lettering. Unlike subsequent orders for coaches and diners, the SOUTHERNER and TENNESSEAN cars carried names as well as road numbers. The TENNESSEAN opened for business as a thirteen-car train that included in its consist a 10-section-3 double bedroom sleeper that operated between Washington and Memphis, and two 12-section-1 drawing room cars that ran Bristol-Nashville and Chattanooga-Memphis. The sleepers were heavyweight cars that had been painted silver to match the exterior appearance of the rest of the train, as Southern did not acquire lightweight sleepers until 1949. Following a brief publicity tour, the TENNESSEAN began revenue service on May 17, 1941.

The divided coaches, peculiar to passenger trains that operated in the deep South, are of some interest. Dating from the Supreme Court's *Plessy v. Ferguson* decision in 1896, "separate but equal" was the law of the land with regard to public accommodations for black and white Americans. However, the situation was especially acute in the Old Confederacy, where states had passed a number of laws intended to institutionalize racial segregation. Included in these "Jim Crow" laws (named for a character made up in black face who appeared in traveling minstrel shows during the late Nineteenth Century) were provisions for separate "white" and "colored" hotels, restaurants and schools, separate theater seating, waiting rooms in train and bus depots, drinking fountains, Bibles for swearing in court witnesses, and, of course, separate seating areas on trains and buses. By law, railroads operating in these states had to include either a separate "colored" coach in their consists, or partitioned coaches that could seat colored riders in one section and white riders in another. In the case of divided coaches, this also meant vestibules at both ends of the car, and a second set of lavatories.

Dining car seating was even more awkward. Under Southern Railway operating rules, dining car crews were directed to curtain off one fourplace table so that colored passengers could eat their meals out of sight of white passengers. However, if the colored table were unoccupied, white patrons could use that table if no others were available. The reverse, however, was not the case. Colored passengers could not eat at a "white" table, even if it was unoccupied and no other "colored" dining tables were available.

In truth, whatever may have been the feelings of individual employees regarding segregation, Jim Crow laws were never very popular with the railroads themselves. For one thing, the requirement to provide separate accommodations for passengers of color often meant having to include extra equipment in the train's consist, not an insignificant consideration during steam days when even a single additional car could tax the capacity of small locomotives. For another, Jim Crow restrictions put railroad crew members in the uncomfortable position of having to act as law enforcement officers. Lastly, there was the threat of legal action. Especially during the war years, railroads frequently found themselves in law courts and ICC hearing rooms defending themselves against complaints filed by African-Americans justifiably upset at being treated as second-class citizens even as they were being charged full-priced fares.

In June 1950, the United States Supreme Court, ruling on a suit filed in 1942, declared discrimination in railroad dining cars unconstitutional. Subsequent Supreme Court rulings, including a case in 1961 involving the famous "Freedom Riders," finally outlawed segregation in interstate transportation, bringing an end to an embarrassing chapter in railroad history. However, the Court's ruling did not end the careers of the divided coaches, which continued in service, but no longer with any restriction on who sat where.

Along with the new streamlined cars, Southern also purchased Electro-Motive E6A passenger diesels 2800-2802 as power for the new SOUTHERNER. At the same time, four E6AB sets were acquired to dieselize the New York-New Orleans CRESCENT, and to provide power for the Bristol-Memphis leg of the TENNESSEAN.

BELOW • *When all the world was young, Southern issued hand-tinted postcards such as these, featuring the new TENNESSEAN and SOUTHERNER streamliners.*

These were units 2900A-2903A and 2900B-2903B. Between Bristol and Lynchburg, Virginia, the TENNESSEAN, along with the workhorse New York-New Orleans PELICAN and the New York-Birmingham BIRMINGHAM SPECIAL, operated over Norfolk & Western iron and ran behind N&W steam. (The actual interchange point for motive power was Monroe, Virginia, eight miles north of Lynchburg.) Back on Southern rails for the short run between Washington and Lynchburg, the TENNESSEAN was headed by Southern's unique Otto Kuhler-styled streamlined PS-4 Pacific 1380. This was because the railroad did not wish to dedicate a scarce diesel to such a short run. However, both the Pacific and the diesels were painted in Southern's attractive green-aluminum-gold livery.

The TENNESSEAN and SOUTHERNER train sets turned out to be the only streamlined equipment acquired by Southern until after V-J Day. America's entry into World War II following the Japanese attack on Pearl Harbor and subsequent War Production Board limitations on the use of steel precluded any possibility of expanding the fleet. However, even without new passenger equipment, the war years were prosperous for Southern. According to figures reported in *Railway Age* in early 1946, overall company revenue in 1945, including Southern, Alabama Great Southern, New Orleans & Northeastern, Georgia Southern & Florida and CNO&TP, totaled $318.6 million, including passenger revenue of $74 million. Net operating income for the year was more than $42 million.

POSTWAR MODERNIZATION

Southern's next venture into the streamlined equipment market came in 1946, when the company and its operating partners ordered lightweight 141 additional cars to re-equip the New York-New Orleans CRESCENT and the Cincinnati-Jacksonville NEW ROYAL PALM. Due to a postwar backlog at all three major car builders, Southern's new equipment was not delivered until late 1949 and early 1950. In the interim the company continued to operate with its existing fleet of aging, but always well-maintained, heavyweight cars.

Connecting and through-car service for Southern passenger trains between Washington and New York was provided by the Pennsylvania Railroad via a hand-off at Washington Union Station. Kansas City and St. Louis connections were with the Frisco at Birmingham Terminal Station. Through car service between Cincinnati and the upper Midwest was with the New York Central. Florida service beyond Jacksonville was provided by the Florida East Coast and the Seaboard Air Line.

Total cost for the 1946 equipment order was $11.5 million. However, because not enough streamlined cars were ordered to re-outfit Southern's secondary mainline trains, in 1947 the company also invested more than $500,000 refurbishing 24 prewar heavyweight coach cars. Included in the upgrade were air conditioning, reclining seats, Thermopane windows and other modern amenities. Externally, however, the refurbished cars remained Pullman green. Two years later, Southern spent another $1.5 million to refurbish 76 additional heavyweights, including 41 coaches, 14 combines, 17 diners and four coach-dinettes. The work was performed at company shops in Chattanooga and Spartanburg. Shop forces did their work well, as many of these veterans continued in secondary service until 1976.

Since the trains being re-equipped ran over several roads between their end points, ownership of the cars was distributed among the various railroads involved. For example, along with cars purchased by Southern, the order for new CRESCENT equipment also included baggage-mail cars lettered or sub lettered for the Western of Alabama and Louisville & Nashville, baggage-dormitory cars for the L&N, coaches for the Atlanta & West Point, L&N and Western of Alabama, and diners for the A&WP and L&N. NEW ROYAL PALM equipment included cars lettered for Southern and Florida East Coast. Operating partner New York Central contributed lightweight cars from its existing pool for NEW ROYAL PALM operations. Postwar cars were built by American Car & Foundry (head-end cars, coaches and diners), The Budd Company (coaches, diners and lounges) and Pullman-Standard (head-end cars and coaches).

In addition to coaches and dining cars, Southern also purchased a number of lightweight sleeping cars for its featured overnight trains. Between September and October 1949, Pullman-Standard delivered forty-six 10-6 cars in the *River* series. Twenty-eight of these were assigned to the flagship CRESCENT. Reflecting the train's participating carriers, cars 2002-2022 were acquired by Southern. Cars 3400 and 3401 were purchased by the L&N, and cars 8351-8358 went to the Pennsylvania. Atlanta & West Point took delivery of *Chattahoochee River* and Western of Alabama took *Alabama River*. Neither the W of A nor the A&WP cars wore a road number at the time of delivery.

Southern also purchased thirteen *River* cars for the NEW ROYAL PALM, numbered in the 2000 and 3400 series. As part of the same order, Florida East Coast acquired exotically named cars *Argentina*, *Brazil*, *Chile*, *Guatemala* and *Venezuela*. As delivered, none of the FEC cars displayed road numbers.

To supplement the 10-6 sleepers, Southern also ordered eleven 14 roomette-4 double bedroom sleepers. Numbered 2200-2210, the 14-4 cars were built to Plan 4135C in Lot 6814 and were named in the *Valley* series. Feature cars for the CRESCENT and NEW ROYAL PALM included eight 5 double bedroom-lounge-observation cars in the *Royal* series and four 1 master room-2 drawing room buffet-lounge cars in the *Crescent* series. The *Royal* cars were built with oversized windows in the observation section, providing an uncommonly scenic ride during the daylight portion of the trip. Ownership of the feature cars was divided among Southern, L&N, Western of Alabama, Florida East Coast and New York Central. Typical of passenger equipment of the era, the passenger compartments of Southern's new cars were decorated in pastel shades of blue, green and tan, and featured themed bulkhead murals in lounges and dining cars. (NOTE: For more complete details on streamlined car names and numbers, delivery dates, etc., see Appendix A at the end of this volume.)

At the same time it was buying cars, Southern was also aggressively replacing steam power with diesel locomotives. Following the 1941 order for EMD E6 passenger locomotives, SR ordered 21 E7A units in 1946 and seven more in 1949, 19 E8As in 1951 and 1953 and 20 FP7s in 1950. The company also acquired three Alco DL109s in 1941 and 1942, and six Alco PA3 units in 1953. Unhappily for Alco fans, the Schenectady-built units suffered from high maintenance expense and enjoyed comparatively short service lives.

In addition to the "pure" passenger units, Southern also amassed a sizable fleet of dual service locomotives, including steam boiler-equipped Alco RS2s (18) and RS3s (27) as well as EMD GP7s (25), FTBs (6), F3As (32), F3Bs (25), F7As ((5) and F7Bs (15). Only a relative few of these units, however, held down regular passenger assignments. Many, in fact, had their steam generators removed in the late 1950s and early 1960s, as passenger operations went into decline. (A complete roster of Southern diesel passenger power is included in Appendix B.)

During the immediate postwar period, Southern fielded an extensive network of mainline trains, including:

NUMBERS	TRAIN NAME	OPERATING BETWEEN
1-2	PONCE DE LEON	Chicago-St. Petersburg
3-4	ROYAL PALM	Chicago-St. Petersburg
5-6	NEW ROYAL PALM	Chicago/Detroit/Buffalo/Cleveland-Miami (seasonal)
7-8	KANSAS CITY-FLORIDA SPECIAL	Kansas City-Jacksonville
9-10	SKYLAND SPECIAL	Asheville-St. Petersburg
15-31-16-32	ASHEVILLE SPECIAL	New York-Asheville
17-18	BIRMINGHAM SPECIAL	New York-Birmingham
21-22	(NORTH) CAROLINA SPECIAL	Chicago-Goldsboro
27-28	(SOUTH) CAROLINA SPECIAL	Chicago-Asheville
29-30	PEACH QUEEN	New York-Atlanta
29-30	SUNNYLAND	St. Louis-Atlanta
31-32	AIKEN-AUGUSTA SPECIAL	New York-Augusta
33-34	PIEDMONT LIMITED	New York-New Orleans
35-36	WASHINGTON-ATLANTA-NEW ORLEANS EXPRESS	Washington-New Orleans
37-38	CRESCENT	New York-New Orleans
39		New York-Atlanta
40	NEW YORKER	Atlanta-New York
41-42	PELICAN	New York-New Orleans
45-46	TENNESSEAN	New York-Memphis
47-48	SOUTHERNER	New York-New Orleans

The Postwar Crescent

Though not the first Southern passenger train to receive lightweight equipment, the unquestioned flagship of the fleet was Trains 37-38, THE CRESCENT LIMITED (known after April 30, 1938 as simply the CRESCENT). The CRESCENT traced its origins to the WASHINGTON AND SOUTHWESTERN VESTIBULED LIMITED of 1891, which ran between the nation's capital and Atlanta. True to its name, the VESTIBULED LIMITED was the first all-season train in the south to carry a complete consist of vestibuled cars. For a $6 extra fare, passengers were treated to a train of "magnificent Pullman Palaces," including drawing room, dining, sleeping, and library cars. The operation was soon expanded to include a through Pullman to Montgomery, Mobile and New Orleans via the Atlanta & West Point, Western of Alabama and Louisville & Nashville. Total running time over the 1,350 mile run was 40 hours, including a connection with the Pennsylvania's CONGRESSIONAL LIMITED in Washington.

The first run of the CRESCENT LIMITED took place on April 26, 1925, with departures from Southern's Canal Street Station in New Orleans and Penn Station in New York City. The all-Pullman CRESCENT operated over the rails of the Louisville & Nashville, Atlanta & West Point, Southern and Pennsylvania, and charged an extra fare (a flat $5 New York to New Orleans) for deluxe service. In all, five complete sets of equipment protected the schedule and employed a crew of 130 (26 for each train), including a valet and a ladies, maid.

The livery of the heavyweight CRESCENT LIMITED was a striking combination of Virginia (dark) and sylvan (light) green trimmed in genuine gold leaf. Cars were named for noteworthy sons of the South, including Confederate General Pierre G. T. Beauregard and storyteller Joel Chandler Harris ("Uncle Remus"). Somewhat confusingly, car names were changed every so often, presumably to spread the honorific further. Prior to delivery of the E6s, power for the CRESCENT was furnished by Southern's famed Ps-4 heavy Pacific steam locomotives, also painted in Virginia green and gold. Unlike the cars, Southern's passenger locomotives were not named.

Except for the change from steam to diesel power in 1941, the CRESCENT carried on as a spit-and-polish heavyweight operation until the arrival of the second batch of streamlined equipment in 1949-1950. After re-equipping, the CRESCENT remained a featured part of Southern's fleet until the late 1960s. By the end of the decade, however, it had lost its status as the road's premiere train, that mantle having passed to the newer, expanded-service SOUTHERNER. Following the loss of its mail contract, the southbound CRESCENT was combined in November 1967 with the SOUTHERNER between Washington and Atlanta, in effect, ceasing to exist as a separate train east of Atlanta. To balance motive power requirements, nameless Train 36, an Atlanta-New York coach-and-mail train that had recently lost most of its head-end business, was discontinued. Additional restructuring followed two years later.

In mid-1969, through car service between Atlanta and New Orleans was eliminated, making the CRESCENT essentially an Atlanta-Washington operation, with cross-platform connections at Terminal Station. Even this last vestige of the glory days ended on January 7, 1970, when the Atlanta & West Point discontinued its coach-only Atlanta-Montgomery remnant. Less than a month later, Southern took steps of its own to rationalize its remaining service. Effective February 1, 1970, the CRESCENT and Train 29, the scruffy PEACH QUEEN were combined between Washington and Atlanta, numbered 5-6 and renamed the PIEDMONT. As the PIEDMONT, the train soldiered on in increasingly diminished form until November 1976, when it was finally discontinued.

The SOUTHERNER, meanwhile, was renumbered 1-2, renamed the SOUTHERN CRESCENT and given management's full attention as SR spared no effort to make the new train a first-rate operation in every regard. On October 19, 1970, the CRESCENT gained a unique new feature when it added to its consist a New York-Los Angeles sleeper that ran three times a week in cooperation with Southern Pacific's SUNSET LIMITED. The coast-to-coast car, and the SOUTHERN CRESCENT alike survived well beyond Amtrak conveyance day on May 1, 1971. Until its eventual hand over to Amtrak in February 1979, Trains 1-2 ran as the showpiece of the railroad, attracting incalculable good will and treating hundreds of thousands of riders to a taste of what passenger trains were like during the "golden age" of the streamliner. At the time of its discontinuance as a Southern operation, the SOUTHERN CRESCENT was still widely acclaimed as the best passenger train in America.

ABOVE • *Here's something you don't see every day! An Alco DL109/DL110 duo leads Train 33, the PIEDMONT LIMITED south of Charlottesville, Virginia in the summer of 1942. During this period, the PIEDMONT was a Washington-New Orleans operation that carried coaches as well as a Washington-Atlanta club car, a New York-New Orleans observation-lounge, a dining car between Atlanta-Montgomery and sleepers from D. C. and New York to Atlanta, Charlotte, Raleigh-Durham and New Orleans. Despite today's assignment to the PIEDMONT, the usual beat for the DLs (as well as the PAs that followed) was the run between Memphis and Bristol.*
(Collection of Jim Neubauer)

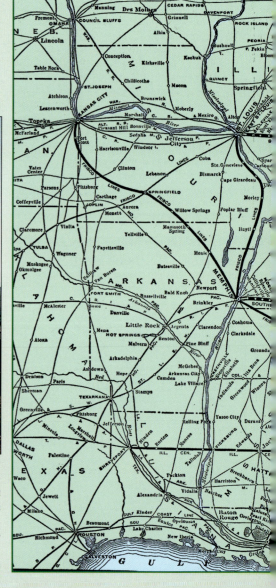

RIGHT • *During the steam era, Southern rostered several classes of Ps-type Pacific passenger locomotives. Not quite as flashy as the famous Ps4 heavy Pacifics, but just as workmanlike, Ps3 Pacifics like New Orleans & North Eastern 6976 toiled on the head end of Southern's passenger trains for more than thirty years. Number 6976 was one of five Ps3s built in 1919, and differed from the more common Ps2s in that they had 68" drivers instead of 72-1/2" for the Ps2 and weighed 209,500 pounds vs. 232,000 for the Ps2. In this photo, one of the company's green-boilered gems smokes it up at Southern's Canal Street Station in New Orleans on September 5, 1943.*
(Shelby F. Lowe, Morning Sun Books Collection)

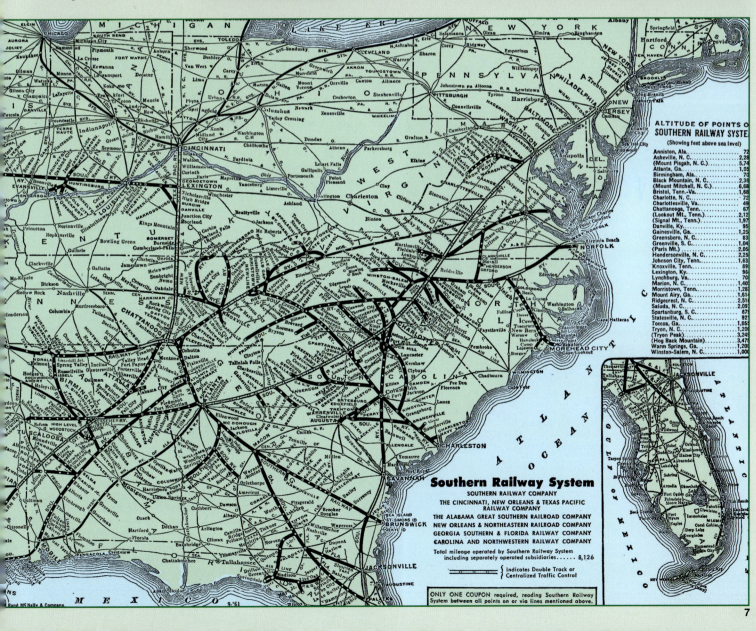

ABOVE • Streamlined Ps4 1380 has strayed a little way off its original patch in this August 1947 view at Atlanta. The streamlined Pacific was built at Alco's Schenectady plant in 1923, had 27" x 28" cylinders and rode on 73" drivers. In 1941 it was streamlined by noted industrial designer Otto Kuhler for duty on the Washington-Monroe, Virginia leg of the new TENNESSEAN. By the date of this photo, however, the one-of-a-kind locomotive had found its way into the general service pool. The beautiful Pacific was sold to scrapper Baltimore Steel in 1953.

(Shelby F. Lowe, Morning Sun Books Collection)

LEFT • Advertisement from 1951 featuring the all-coach version of the new SOUTHERNER.

BELOW • At the time Southern first went shopping for diesels, it specified an attractive green and imitation aluminum livery trimmed with gold striping. In this 1947 scene, nearly-brand-new F3s 4131 and 4133 bask in the sun at Washington, DC. As things turned out, these two units enjoyed long careers. Upgraded to 1,500 horsepower in 1951, no. 4131 remained in service until 1963; 4133 lasted even longer, sticking around until 1972, an incredible 26 years! *(Collection of Jim Neubauer)*

ABOVE • By the early 1920s, the 4-6-2 Pacific-type had become the standard passenger locomotive on the Southern Railway. However, early versions such as Ps 1240, shown here enjoying the summer sunshine at Charleston, South Carolina in the late 1940's, proved too light for Southern's big trains and were supplanted later in the decade by the heavier Ps4s. Quite possibly the train we are looking at here is No. 12, a local that ran between Charleston and Branchville, SC.

(Nelson Bowers photo)

ABOVE • When Southern needed to get a heavy train over the hill, it called on one of its class Ts1 4-8-2 Mountains. Working primarily out of mountain-area terminals such as Knoxville and Asheville, the big haulers were built with 68" drivers (compared to 73" for the Ps4 Pacifics) and generated 53,900 pounds of tractive effort vs. 47500 pounds for the Pacifics. As such, they were the obvious choice outside the "flatlands" south of Chattanooga. Here, No. 1487 steams easily at Asheville, North Carolina. All of the handsome Mountains met the scrapper's torch during the early 1950s. (Gray Lackey Collection)

Above • Pacific 1390 strikes a classic "rods down" pose on an overcast afternoon at Washington, D. C. in September 1948. The Ps4 is now in its third decade of service, having rolled out of Alco's Schenectady shops in 1924. Other members of the graduating class include SR 1366-1374, 1387-1389 and 1391-1409 as well as Cincinnati, New Orleans & Texas Pacific 6471-6475 and Alabama Great Southern 6684-6691. Eventually, Southern would roster 64 of the USRA design Ps4s, one of which, no. 1401, wound up being donated in 1962 for display at the Smithsonian Institution in Washington, D. C. *(Bill Ellis photo)*

Above • *National Geographic* advertisement from April 1946.

Above • By 1949, diesels were making definite inroads into Southern's passenger locomotive fleet. One early example is F3A 4134, accompanied by an unidentified F3B mate at Alexandria, Virginia, as its train loads a hefty stack of mail. The F3 rolled out of EMD's LaGrange, Illinois factory in 1946 and ended up spending the next 26 years toiling in Southern service. Along the way, the unit underwent a number of changes, including upgrading to F7 rating in 1950 and the installation of dynamic brakes and roof air tanks in 1954. *(Steve Bogen photo)*

ABOVE • You have to look closely, but there's a lot to see in this photo, taken at D. C.'s Ivy City engine terminal on September 1, 1951. In addition to Southern E7 2917, there's Richmond, Fredericksburg & Potomac boiler-equipped GP7 101 and Chesapeake & Ohio streamlined 4-6-4 490. The Hudson and three mates were rebuilt and restyled in 1946-1947 from 1926-model F-19 Pacifics to power connecting sections of C&O's stillborn CHESSIE, which was planned to run between Washington and Cincinnati.

(Dr. L. H. Leggett photo, William Shoemaker Collection)

ABOVE • Here's another look at Pacific 1380. Built in 1923, 1380 worked in general passenger service until 1941 when it was tapped to head the streamlined TENNESSEAN, operated jointly with the Norfolk & Western. When it returned to the general passenger pool in the late 1940s, 1380 retained its green and white shrouding and TENNESSEAN lettering, but spent the rest of its days hauling secondary passenger runs. By that time, shiny new diesels had grabbed the spotlight.

(Dr. L. H. Leggett photo, William Shoemaker Collection)

ABOVE • No longer resplendent in its original green and aluminum paint, Southern Train No. 20, the GOLDENROD rattles into Mobile, Alabama in the early 1950s. The GOLDENROD and sisters the VULCAN, CRACKER and JOE WHEELER were powered by 800 horsepower Fairbanks-Morse opposed piston diesel engines, more than ample to move their diminutive trains. Always reliable, but never fancy, the GOLDENROD offered coach accommodations only over its 266-mile, 9-hour run. *(Gib Allbach Collection)*

RIGHT • Pullman-Standard ran this promotional piece dating from 1941. The ad was directed at railroad managers, not the traveling public.

LEFT AND BELOW • So when did Southern electrify its Washington-Atlanta main line? Not in your lifetime. In fact, we're looking at CRESCENT No. 38 as it heads north through Greer, South Carolina on June 26, 1950. As a result of a derailment at Lyman, South Carolina on Southern's own main line, the flagship was forced to detour over electric interurban Piedmont & Northern. In this coming-and-going photo sequence, CRESCENT No. 38 heads north at Greer on June 26, 1950.

(S. A. Goodrick photo)

Above • An oddity within the car order for the 1941 SOUTHERNER was that car names appeared on more than one car. For example, there were three 54-seat "Jim Crow" coaches named *South Carolina* (nos. 900-901), two *Georgias*, three *Virginias* and three *Louisianas*, including car 1101, seen here at Pennsylvania's Sunnyside Yard in Long Island, New York on June 14, 1947. All three *Louisianas* were tavern-lounge-observations that included lounge seating on curved settees, tavern seating for sixteen and eighteen seats in the observation. In addition, there was a mid-car buffet and a sleeping compartment for the train hostess.
(Lawson Hill photo, collection of Boston Chapter NRHS)

Above • Pacific 1369 leads a heavyweight train into the depot at Charlotte, North Carolina on June 27, 1950. Although no information is included on the slide, steam power and the length of the surrounding shadows suggests that we're looking at No. 12, the all-stops local from Greenville. *(S. A. Goodrick photo)*

LEFT • Four-year old E7A 2915 idles at Ivy City engine terminal in June 1950. At the time of this photo, the unit was still at the beginning of its long (and occasionally unlucky) career. In 1952, 2915 was rebuilt after being wrecked. It was rebuilt a second time and upgraded to E8 rating (2,250 horsepower) at Spencer shops in August 1954. The unit was retired and returned to EMD for trade-in credit in 1968. *(Dr. L. H. Leggett photo, William Shoemaker Collection)*

LEFT, CENTER • Heavyweight dining car 3169 is open for business on this September 5, 1954 afternoon. 3169 was one of a group of cars (3164-3170) that was upgraded by Southern in the late 1940s as new streamlined cars began to arrive on the property. For many years after they served on Southern's secondary passenger trains, including the PELICAN, BIRMINGHAM SPECIAL, PIEDMONT LIMITED and others. *(Lawson Hill photo, collection of Boston Chapter NRHS)*

BELOW • In the early 1950s, more than 250 passenger trains called each day at Washington Union Station, including those of the Baltimore & Ohio, Chesapeake & Ohio, Pennsylvania, Richmond, Fredericksburg & Potomac/Seaboard/Atlantic Coast Line and, of course, Southern. Located just to the northeast of Union Station was Ivy City Yard and Engine Terminal, where trains and locomotives were serviced and turned. Included in the Ivy City complex were two roundhouses served by two turntables (one each for steam and diesel locomotives) and a 76-track coach yard. In September 1951, Southern, C&O and RF&P power await their next call before heading back out on the road. *(Dr. L. H. Leggett photo, William Shoemaker Collection)*

ABOVE • Considering its status at the nation's second largest rail hub, St. Louis was little more than a backwater as far as Southern passenger service was concerned. Indeed, by 1949, SR was down to local Trains 23-24 between Danville, Kentucky and East St. Louis Relay Depot (in order to save terminal costs, the SR trains did not cross the Mississippi River after September 1948). At Relay, passengers made an across-the-platform connection with GM&O Trains 11-12 for the short hop across into St. Louis. On June 16, 1952, Southern's locals, shown here at Huntingburg, Indiana in August of that year, were cut back to Mt. Carmel, Illinois. Southern passenger service in Indiana lasted until June 30, 1953 and survived for another two years in Kentucky.
(M. D. McCarter photo)

ABOVE • Another look at No. 24 at Huntingburg, Indiana in the summer of 1952. The photo suggests that the little train ran on a fast schedule, but such was not the case. On the 362-mile route between Danville and East St. Louis, 23-24 were carded for 63 positive and conditional stops, and burned almost 13 hours! *(M. D. McCarter photo)*

Above • Not exactly a passenger train, but a photo of some note nevertheless. On November 3, 1952, an A-B-B-A covered wagon set led by F7A 4208 escorts a "funeral train" of 26 steam locomotives through Reidsville, North Carolina. Southern was an early proponent of diesel locomotion, and dropped its fires system-wide on June 17, 1953. Oh, yes, no. 4208 itself went to scrap via a trade-in to EMD in March 1971.
(Shelby F. Lowe, Morning Sun Books Collection)

Above • We're standing on the platform at Asheville in July 1953 looking at what appears to be Train 15, the Washington-Asheville ASHEVILLE SPECIAL. As of this date, the train was still a big one. It included coaches, a Greensboro-Asheville dining car and three sleepers: two lightweight cars to New York and a heavyweight car to Washington. The F3 up front is something of an odd bird, having originally been delivered in 1949 without a steam generator, but modified at Spencer in 1952 to include one.
(Arthur Angstadt, Hawk Mountain Chapter NRHS collection)

Above • Just to look at Central of Georgia E8s 811 and 812, you'd think the 1,800-mile road was a subsidiary of the Baltimore & Ohio. In fact, during the 1950s, the company was aggressively courted by the Frisco, which took a strong equity position. This lasted until 1961, when SLSF was directed by the ICC to divest its holdings. Two years later, on June 17, 1963, the Central of Georgia came under Southern control. About 811 and 812: The pair were the only E8 models owned by Central of Georgia and were eventually used in joint service with the Illinois Central on the Chicago-Florida SEMINOLE and CITY OF MIAMI trains. Central of Georgia also rostered 10 E7s.

(Emery Gulash, Morning Sun Books Collection)

Above • No caption information accompanied this photo of CNO&TP FP7 6137 and a mate on the point of a passenger train during the "green era." Even so, however, the image is instructive. The automobiles parked in the background at right suggest that the photo dates from the late 1950s. The consist of heavyweight equipment trailing the F-units makes this a secondary train, and the long string of head-end cars tells us its primary business is mail and express. *(Preston Johnson photo)*

ABOVE • In August 1946, Southern ordered six chair-lounge cars numbered 950-955 from the Budd Company for use in general service. Due to the crush of wartime backlogs, however, the cars did not arrive on the property until November and December of 1949 (imagine waiting three years for a new car!). As delivered, the cars included coach seating for 34 and a 16-seat bar-lounge area. Later, two pairs of seats were removed to provide space for a conductor's office. The cars survived into the Claytor era, and in 1979 were sold to Amtrak where they were renumbered 3850-3855. A quarter century earlier, car 955 splices an otherwise all-heavyweight consist made up of SR and Norfolk & Western equipment on what appears to be a railfan trip.

(Lawson Hill photo, collection of Boston Chapter NRHS)

ABOVE • E7 2914 and an A-B set of F-unit mates power Train 35, the WASHINGTON- ATLANTA- NEW ORLEANS EXPRESS on the first leg of its southbound journey over Southern rails. The train originated in New York at 12:30 PM and arrived in the nation's capitol at 4:25 PM. After exchanging Pennsy GG1 power for Southern diesels, the EXPRESS was underway again at 4:50 PM. In this photo, dating from September 8, 1956, we catch up with No. 35 as it rolls through Alexandria, Virginia.

(Walter Zullig, Jr. photo)

ABOVE • Today's BIRMINGHAM SPECIAL is running twelve cars long, including a healthy cut of head-end equipment. The appearance of this train is fairly typical of Southern's secondary trains in that its consist includes a mix of streamlined and heavyweight cars. On this September 1956 day the train is powered by an E7 pair led by no. 2917. At Monroe, Virginia, No. 17 will be handed over to the Norfolk & Western, which will substitute steam power for its portion of the run between Monroe and Bristol. *(Walter Zullig, Jr. photo)*

BELOW • Between June 1949 and December 1953, EMD produced 297 1,500 horsepower FP7 units, including Southern 6143 and 6148, shown here at Cincinnati on August 13, 1957. The units can be distinguished from conventional F-units by their additional 4 feet of length, which is most readily visible between the lead truck and the fuel tank. Southern's FP7s were sub lettered for the CNO&TP. Unit 6143 had a particularly long life, remaining on the roster until 1988. Unit 6148 was returned to EMD as a trade-in in 1979. *(David T. Mainey photo)*

Looking like a publicity man's annual report cover photo, Train 18, the northbound BIRMINGHAM SPECIAL climbs an easy grade at Alexandria in the summer of 1956. At Washington, the SPECIAL will turn over its heavyweight sleepers to the Pennsylvania for the remainder of their run to New York City. During this period, Nos. 17-18 handled two daily sleepers, an 8-section sleeper-restaurant lounge and an every third day Pullman between New York and Knoxville.
(Walter Zullig, Jr. photo)

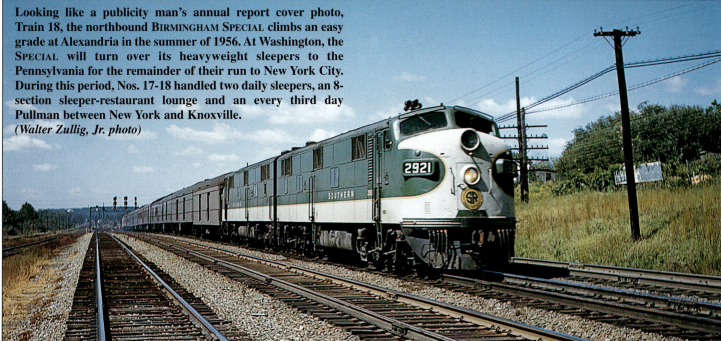

SR 20

LEFT, ABOVE • Signature cars for Trains 37-38, the flagship CRESCENT were four 5 double bedroom-buffet-lounge-observation named in the *Royal* series. The cars were out shopped by Pullman-Standard during February and March of 1950. They were built to Plan 4162, Lot 6814. Car 2300, *Royal Arch*, was delivered to Southern. Two others went to the Louisville & Nashville and one to the Western of Alabama. Four identical cars were built as part of the same lot for the Cincinnati-Jacksonville NEW ROYAL PALM. *(T. J. Donahue photo)*

LEFT, BELOW • It's just after 8:00 in the morning and the hand-off of the CRESCENT from Southern to the West Point Route is underway at Atlanta's Terminal Station in the summer of 1959. The overnight Washington-New Orleans streamliner included coaches, a diner and at least a half-dozen sleepers between New York and New Orleans, including a *Royal*-series observation-lounge. The West Point will turn over the streamliner to Louisville & Nashville for the final leg of the run into New Orleans. If the CRESCENT is on time (and there will be the devil to pay if she's not), her passengers will able to relax over a "Hurricane" cocktail at Pat O'Brien's and still have time for dinner at a civilized hour. *(Collection of Jim Neubauer)*

RIGHT • "Service", "Scenery", "Comfort": The CRESCENT had it all in 1955.

BELOW • A last look at passenger railroading, Southern style, at Alexandria, Virginia in the 1950s. There is no mistaking the pride of the company as it puts its best foot forward with glossy E-units and a matched set of streamlined cars stretching out of sight around the platform. *(T. J. Donahue photo)*

SOUTHERN RAILWAY THROUGH PASSENGER SERVICE 1960-1970: DISILLUSIONMENT AND DECLINE

For American passenger railroads, the decade of the 1950s began with guarded optimism. True enough, ridership had declined significantly from the peak level of the war years. Still, from the railroad's point of view there was still much to feel good about. For one thing, the traveling public seemed to have enthusiastically embraced the new streamliners which had been introduced by just about every major railroad during the immediate postwar period. Also encouraging was the fact that, although the railroads' share of the inter-city passenger business had shrunk to 46.3% (from a high of 77% in 1929, and 74% as late as 1944), the remaining volume seemed to be holding steady. Most carriers still believed, or at least stated for public consumption, that there was a bright future for passenger trains, if only operating expenses could be held in check. Reflecting what, in hindsight, was clearly a heart-over-head attitude, the railroads put their shareholders' money where their publicists' mouths were. Between 1946 and 1950, more than 4,300 new lightweight passenger cars were added to the nation's fleet.

As has been well documented, despite all the glittering new equipment, can-do attitude and upbeat news releases, the effort ultimately came to nothing. During the period 1947-1957, driven primarily by increased wages, the cost to the railroads of providing a mile of passenger transportation increased by a staggering 72%. By 1957, according to Interstate Commerce Commission accounting guidelines, American railroads were losing more than $720 million a year on passenger operations (though far less on an avoidable-cost basis). At the same time, ridership began a steep, eventually fatal, decline. By 1960, the rails' share of the inter-city passenger business had fallen to 29%; in 1970 it hovered just above 7%.

What went wrong? Much has been written concerning this subject, and an in-depth discussion on the demise of the American passenger train is beyond the scope of this volume. Suffice it to say the causes were legion: skyrocketing labor costs; aging, expensive-to-maintain rolling stock and locomotives, more reliable automobiles; the jet airplane; an improved highway system; and government policy which reflected its effect, if not in its intent, a decided bias in favor of the competition.

Consider: After World War II, federal, state and local governments collectively invested billions of dollars in support of the airline industry. In every city big enough to have a stoplight, airports were constructed using tax dollars. Operation of these same airports was then supported by an FAA-managed air traffic control system. Further, in the 1950s, construction began on the federally-funded Interstate Highway System. which was to be the largest federally-funded public works project in history. Eventually, more than 42,000 miles of high-speed, limited access expressways were built, all at taxpayer (including railroads) expense. In addition, government provided a cornucopia of tax breaks to the oil industry to help make sure gasoline prices stayed low, and Detroit assembly lines kept humming..

Finally, it was government, in the character of a cartoon character named Mr. ZIP, that delivered the fatal, if unintentional, blow. In October 1967 the Post Office Department gave the railroads notice of its intention to immediately remove all first-class mail from passenger trains. The plan was to shift first-class mail to the airlines and utilize regional sorting centers (based on ZIP codes) instead of Railway Post Office cars. Railroads would be paid no more than freight rates for moving the remaining third-class (bulk) mail. Losing the mail was devastating, and set in motion a stampede on the part of every railroad in the country to seek permission to eliminate practically all their remaining passenger trains.

Case in point: On December 16, 1949, Southern's winter-season NEW ROYAL PALM made its inaugural departure (taking the place of the heavyweight, seasonal FLORIDA SUNBEAM) from Cincinnati Union Terminal, bound for the sunny climes of Florida's east coast. Included in its consist were through cars gathered by the New York Central, and delivered to the Queen City from such Midwestern cold-weather capitals as Buffalo, Cleveland, Chicago and Detroit. The name "NEW ROYAL PALM" was needed because there was an "old" ROYAL PALM, which had been operating between the Ohio River and Florida since the 1920s. The NEW ROYAL PALM, however, was more than just a replacement. It was new. It was colorful. It was glamorous, and it was a streamliner, designed to complete with established Midwestern Florida streamliners such as Illinois Central's CITY OF MIAMI, Pennsylvania's SOUTH WIND and C&EI's DIXIE FLAGLER. If one were to judge from the promotional campaign sponsored by Southern, no train was ever given a splashier rollout, and by all accounts, THE NEW ROYAL PALM was an instant success.

According to the January 1950 edition of Southern's *Ties* employee magazine, "crowds of people turned out along the train's route," to welcome it at the depot, or just to watch and wave as it passed. In Vero Beach, Florida, more than 1,200 "civic-minded persons" showed up at the station for a christening ceremony. As part of the festivities, a high school band played, souvenir packages of oranges and postcards were distributed and a special "NEW ROYAL PALM EDITION" of the Vero Beach *Press-Journal* was handed out. Capping the day's events, Miss June Zigrang smashed a bottle of orange juice across the pilot of the lead locomotive, and Miss Tracy Kromhout snipped a ribbon stretched across the tracks, sending the train on its way. To help ensure that no aspect of passenger comfort was overlooked, onboard hostesses were assigned to each run of the NEW ROYAL PALM. Those who served included Misses Jane Lanier, Winnie McClellan, Ouida Sue Flynt, Jean Farned and Barbara Rutledge. Overall, passengers described the train as "tops."

So successful was the NEW ROYAL PALM that even in 1955, its final season as a winter-only operation, it was handling no fewer than eight lightweight sleepers (*nine* on Tuesdays, Wednesdays, Fridays and Saturdays) in five different configurations, including 14-4, 10-6, 4-4-2 and 13-double bedroom cars, plus a 5-double bedroom lounge-observation. Also in the consist were streamlined coaches, a coach-lounge and a dining car.

Following the 1955 season, the NEW ROYAL PALM was expanded from a seasonal to a daily operation and its equipment was transferred to the schedule of the "old" ROYAL PALM, which was then discontinued. Sadly, the streamliner's magic did not extend into the 1960s, as low airline fares and the new Interstate Highway System brought Florida closer than ever to Ohio's doorstep.

By the winter of 1961-62, the ROYAL PALM was down to coaches, a single 10-6 sleeper between Cincinnati-Jacksonville, and a diner that ran only as far as Atlanta. No through cars operated beyond Jacksonville or Cincinnati, and even the lone sleeper was gone by 1966. By then, the train had been cut back to the unlikely southern terminus of Valdosta, Georgia. (Trimming trains back to absurd end points was a technique Southern used again and again to discourage ridership and expedite the process of obtaining authorization to discontinue them.) Trains 3-4, the last remnant of the ROYAL PALM, made their final runs on January

31, 1970. At the time, the trains were operating as a Cincinnati-Somerset, Kentucky local that consisted of a coach or two and a baggage car behind FP7 6145.

THE TENNESSEE TRAINS

With the exception of the CRESCENT and the SOUTHERNER, just about every train in Southern's passenger fleet underwent serious downgrading during the late 1950s and early 1960s. Although it has been argued that Southern's varnish was more than paying its way, the attitude of the company's management toward its passenger trains had soured, and it began taking drastic steps to reduce expenses. The result was that what had previously been a fleet of full-service trains turned quickly into little more than a collection of bare-bones mail and express runs.

To illustrate, in 1949 Southern, in cooperation with the Norfolk & Western, was fielding three pairs of passenger trains daily over their end-to-end lines extending through western Virginia and eastern Tennessee. These were Trains 17-18, the BIRMINGHAM SPECIAL, between Washington and Birmingham; Trains 45-46, the Washington-Memphis TENNESSEAN; and Trains 41-42, the Washington-New Orleans PELICAN. None of the trains were "pure" streamliners, and, except for the TENNESSEAN, none regularly carried more than one or two lightweight cars. All three trains began to unravel at about the same time as the ROYAL PALM, and with one exception, all were dead and buried by the time Amtrak took over most of America's remaining passenger trains in May 1971.

In the summer of 1955, the BIRMINGHAM SPECIAL was a real-deal train. It carried coaches and sleepers between Washington and Birmingham, a 10-6 lightweight Pullman and a heavyweight restaurant-lounge-sleeper between New York City and Birmingham. Also in its consist was a heavyweight Washington-Knoxville sleeper, and a Washington-Roanoke dining car. At Chattanooga, the SPECIAL connected with all-stops local Trains 35-36. These provided service to and from Memphis on a nine-hour daylight carding, running essentially opposite the much more up-market TENNESSEAN. So far, so good, but reductions were not long in coming. By 1956, the SPECIAL had been trimmed back to a single Washington-Birmingham sleeper. Five years later the sleeper was running only as far as Chattanooga, making the train coach-only the rest of the way to Birmingham.

By the summer of 1965, the BIRMINGHAM SPECIAL had become decidedly un-special. The train was down to a couple of the rebuilt heavyweight coaches, plus a clutch of mail-storage cars over the length of the run between Washington and Birmingham. Public timetables dating from 1969 show the return of a Washington-Monroe dining car, but this was gone by 1971. Before that time, however, the train had been discontinued within the state of Tennessee. On August 11, 1970, the SPECIAL was cut back to Washington-Bristol (Virginia) and Valley Head-Birmingham, Alabama. Unable to attract any sort of meaningful ridership, the Alabama stub train was discontinued shortly thereafter.

Amazingly, however, as a coach-only Washington-Bristol train, Nos. 17-18 survived into the Amtrak era. After May 1, 1971, the N&W portion of the run was eliminated by Amtrak. Southern, however, by virtue of the fact that it chose not to become part of Amtrak, was obliged to retain the Lynchburg-Washington stub until at least January 1, 1975. For much of that time the train was almost unrecognizable as a passenger train. It consisted of a single modernized heavyweight coach and an FP7 sandwiched for almost the entire length of its run into the consist of a piggyback train. Operating as Trains 7-8, the skeleton of the old BIRMINGHAM SPECIAL made its last run in the summer of 1975.

With considerable fanfare, the streamlined TENNESSEAN entered service on May 18, 1941, as a replacement for the heavyweight MEMPHIS SPECIAL. As was customary for new streamlined trains, the TENNESSEAN was dispatched on a promotional tour before entering revenue service. According to literature of the period, the tour was a huge success. Between Memphis and Lynchburg alone, more than 100,000 people toured the train, including more than 43,000 in Virginia. Once in service, the TENNESSEAN proved even more popular. Despite being only slightly faster than the train it replaced (due to its extensive mail-handling chores), coach patronage more than doubled during the first six months of operation.

Although there was some minor downgrading during the early part of the decade, (the observation car was eliminated in 1954), TENNESSEAN service held up reasonably well throughout the 1950s. In 1955, dining car service was still available between Washington and Knoxville (it had originally run as far as Chattanooga), a restaurant-lounge-sleeper was open for business between Chattanooga and Memphis, and a New York-Memphis 14-4 lightweight sleeper was offered. There was even a Bristol-Nashville Pullman that was handled west of Chattanooga by Nashville, Chattanooga & St. Louis Trains 3-4. It was in this form that the TENNESSEAN rolled into the decade of the New Frontier.

To understand what happened to the TENNESSEAN, it is important to understand that its *real* business (like that of the MEMPHIS SPECIAL it replaced) was handling the mail, and it was the train's mail contract that was its principal source of revenue. Thus, any money that could be saved by reducing passenger service costs went straight to the company's bottom line. And so, as ridership began to decline,

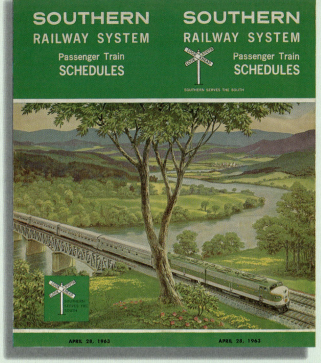

ABOVE • *Southern's Spring 1963 timetable was still thick, but many of the trains listed carried far more mail than passengers.*

downgrading began in earnest. In 1964, dining car service was cut back to Bristol-Roanoke. By the following year the TENNESSEAN was down to a single Knoxville-Memphis 10-6 sleeper.

At the same time, Southern's D. W. Brosnan-led management team determined that current levels of ridership no longer supported three passenger trains through Tennessee, and that most of the mail revenue could be retained if one train was eliminated. Accordingly, on June 27, 1966, the TENNESSEAN and the PELICAN were combined into a single operation as far as Chattanooga. To implement the restructuring, the consolidated train ran on the schedule of the PELICAN. By this time, of course, Southern, like many other railroads, was doing everything it could to minimize passenger operating expenses. According to an ICC report filed the following year, SR lost more than $16 million on its passenger trains in 1966 alone.

Like the BIRMINGHAM SPECIAL, the PELICAN was a mostly heavyweight train. In the late 1940s, it was also a *big* train: Two 10-2 sleepers between New York and New Orleans; a 12-1 sleeper between New York and Shreveport (via a connection with the Illinois Central at Meridian, Mississippi); a New York-Williamson, West Virginia 10-6 lightweight sleeper (via N&W's CAVALIER at Roanoke); a New York-Bristol 10-2 car; a Washington-New Orleans 12-section lounge; and 12-1 cars between Washington-Roanoke and Atlanta-Shreveport, the second of which was handled by the PELICAN between Meridian and Birmingham. The trains also carried head end cars plus coaches and an N&W dining car that ran between Roanoke and Birmingham.

During the 1950s, PELICAN passenger loads held up considerably better than those of its stable mates on the route. In 1955, for example, Nos. 41-42 still handled six sleepers (compared to three for the BIRMINGHAM SPECIAL and four for the TENNESSEAN), including cars between Washington-Shreveport, Washington-Roanoke and between New York and Bristol, Knoxville, New Orleans and Williamson. Speed was not a primary selling point, as the trains ran over the 1,115.7 mile run on a 30-hour schedule designed around the needs of the Post Office and not the traveling public. Nevertheless, the service held up reasonably well for the rest of the decade. Times, however, were a-changing.

By the early 1960s, the PELICAN was slipping badly. In 1961 the first-class portion of the train was cut back to a pair of 10-6 sleepers between New York-New Orleans and New York-Bristol, plus head-end cars, coaches, and the Roanoke-Birmingham dining car. In 1963, sleeping car service was eliminated south of Chattanooga. And in 1965, the dining car, by this time cut back to Roanoke-Bristol, was available southbound only.

As mentioned above, in June 1966, the PELICAN and the TENNESSEAN were combined between Washington and Chattanooga. The new operation carried timetable numbers 41-45 and 46-42 and was renamed the PELICAN-TENNESSEAN over the portion of the route where they ran as a single train. Despite indications that both trains were covering at least their direct costs of operation, Southern and Norfolk & Western claimed in their briefs before state regulators that the consolidation the PELICAN and the TENNESSEAN across the state of Virginia would result in an annual savings of $640,000.

For a short time, the main stem of the PELICAN-TENNESSEAN retained a vestige of style, at least on the Virginia end of its route. Riders could reserve space aboard a 10-6 sleeper between New York and Chattanooga, and could grab an early dinner in an N&W dining car between Bristol and Roanoke (for all three of the "Tennessee trains," N&W appeared to be the more conscientious of the operating partners with respect to maintaining amenities). West of Chattanooga, over the daylight portion of the run, however, the PELICAN took on the ratty appearance of every other Southern secondary passenger train: a coach or two, three head end cars and FP7 power.

In early 1967, Memphis-Chattanooga local trains were discontinued and what was left of the once-proud TENNESSEAN became the last train on the route. Running on a graveyard schedule, the TENNESSEAN remnant rolled into Memphis at an ungodly 2:00 AM. Departure time for eastbound No. 46 was an equally customer-unfriendly 11:00 PM. By this time, the TENNESSEAN name had been eliminated from public timetables. With little patronage to support it, Nos. 45-46 lasted a while longer, until the loss of its mail contract spelled the end of the line in March 1968.

For the PELICAN, further cutbacks followed. In June 1968 the train was no longer running through to New Orleans. Instead, without opposition from either the states of Mississippi or Louisiana, the southern terminus was changed to York, Alabama, the last scheduled stop east of the Mississippi state line. Dining car service remained on the N&W portion of the route, and the 10-6 sleeper continued to run between Washington and Bristol. However, in April 1969 the Bristol-Chattanooga leg was dropped, orphaning the Alabama end of the run until it was finally discontinued in September of that year.

In December 1969, Southern undertook a general renumbering of its remaining passenger trains (except for Nos. 17-18), with the remnant of the PELICAN emerging as Trains 11-12. On August 2, 1970, Norfolk & Western discontinued its portion of the run between Lynchburg and Bristol. Nine days later, on August 11, the trains made their final runs between Washington and Lynchburg, eliminating the operation altogether.

ABOVE • *In the early 1960s, Southern passenger service into Memphis consisted of nameless Chattanooga-Memphis locals 35-36, and the featured Washington-Memphis Trains 45-46, the TENNESSEAN. In this photo from the period, E6 2800 receives a quick once-over at Memphis Union Station as it awaits its next assignment. Interestingly, 2800 was the very first E-unit acquired by Southern, arriving on the property in March 1941 as power for the all-new SOUTHERNER. This unit had quite a long career, remaining on the roster until August 1967, when it returned to EMD as a trade-in.* (Emery Gulash, Morning Sun Books Collection)

ABOVE • *Southern operated a large fleet of business cars that roamed from one end of the system to the other. Here's Car 11 at the brand-new Roanoke, Virginia passenger depot (on the Norfolk & Western) in July 1962. On this particular afternoon, Car 11 is carrying the markers of Train 42, the Washington-New Orleans* PELICAN.

(Gib Allbach Collection)

ABOVE • *Coupled to an Alco switcher, Southern PA3 6902 catches some late afternoon sunshine at Chattanooga, Tennessee. Always popular with railfans, the six 2,250 horsepower units were purchased in a single lot in late 1953. Alas, Southern's experience with the Alcos was similar to that of many other railroads. High maintenance expense, particularly with the crankshafts of the 244-series prime movers, led to the the Alcos, retirement en masse in 1965. Southern owned only three other Also passenger units, a trio of DL-109s delivered in 1941.*

(Morning Sun Books Collection)

Above • Frisco E8 units 2011 and 2012 lead the Kansas City-Florida Special at Amory, Mississippi on a sweltering July 20, 1962. At one time, Frisco and Southern operated a thriving joint passenger business between Kansas City, St. Louis and Jacksonville, Florida. By the date of this photo, however, through car service was down to Kansas City-Jacksonville coaches and a single Frisco 14-4 sleeper. SLSF 105-106 also offered a lounge and a diner on this train, but neither car operated beyond Birmingham. Frisco's other Kansas City-Birmingham train, Nos. 101-102 offered no through cars, but did advertise a connection with the Seaboard for coach service into Atlanta. *(Louis A. Marre photo)*

Left • A nearly matched set of E-units (Southern did not roster any of EMD's comparatively rare E8Bs) cruise past the headquarters of Atlanta-based office supply giant S. P. Richards in September 1962. From the position of the sun, it's a good guess that this is power for Number 38, the Crescent, due out of Atlanta 12:35 PM, or Number 30, the Peach Queen, carded for a 1:30 PM departure. By the early 1960s, the original green paint on Southern passenger power was fast becoming a memory, covered over by a more somber, but still reasonably stylish, black/white/gold. *(Collection of Matthew Herson)*

Above • Same time, same place, question answered. Since this is obviously *not* the Crescent, it must be the Peach Queen, bound for a 6:40 AM next-day arrival Washington. Southern was an early proponent of adding piggyback (and sometimes other freight equipment) to passenger trains in an effort to squeeze every possible dollar out of a train-mile. Further up the line, No. 30 will pick up New York-bound sleepers in Greenville, Charlotte and Winston-Salem. For now, though, she's not much more than a glorified mixed train.

(Collection of Matthew Herson)

Left • It's 3:50 on a hazy September 1962 afternoon as Number 38, the northbound Crescent, pays a call at Greenville, South Carolina. During this period, the Crescent handled at least six sleepers into Washington, including a 10-6 car that was added in Greenville. A second 10-6 will be tacked on at Charlotte. As Southern's route east of Atlanta was mountainous, there are three E-units up front. On the relatively flat terrain across Alabama and Mississippi, the Crescent usually ran behind paired FP7s on the A&WP and Western of Alabama, and a couple of E-units on the Louisville & Nashville. *(Collection of Matt Herson)*

ABOVE • Southern owned only a handful of lightweight baggage and express cars, so most trains included a cut of heavyweights on the head end. Car in point: baggage-express 121, seen here at Pennsylvania's Spruce Street Coach Yard in Columbus, Ohio in December 1962. Car 121 was 61 feet in length and rode on four-wheel trucks. It was lettered for Railway Express duty, which often led the car far from home rails. That star above the batten strip indicates that this is a messenger car, and includes a small desk and a toilet for an agent, who worked the car en route. *(Paul Winters photo)*

ABOVE • Pride of the fleet! Spanking-clean E8 6913 and a matched stainless consist mark this train as Number 48, the SOUTHERNER, seen here at New Orleans on April 20, 1963. On its overnight run to Washington, the SOUTHERNER will get progressively longer as it makes its way north: Two coaches and one sleeper added in Birmingham, a tavern-lounge picked up in Atlanta, two more sleepers added at Asheville. Hence, this six-car job leaving NOUPT at 7:30 AM will swell into twelve cars more by the time it makes its final sprint into DC. Oh, yes, with all those extra cars, she'll also add another E-unit or two in Atlanta.

(J. W. Swanberg photo)

ABOVE • It may not be much to look at, but this train is a moneymaker! Number 42, the northbound New Orleans-Washington PELICAN pauses at Chattanooga on a gloomy September 14, 1963. Like her sisters on the run through Tennessee, the primary job of Nos. 41-42 was toting the mail, as evidenced by the lengthy string of head-end equipment. By this time, however, the usual passenger portion of the train was down to a pair of 10-6 sleepers (New York-New Orleans and New York-Bristol), a Roanoke-Knoxville dining car and a cut of modernized heavyweight coaches. *(Walter E. Zullig photo)*

ABOVE • Five stainless cars are sandwiched between a long cut of SR heavyweight cars and a single Pennsylvania sleeper as Train 4, the northbound ROYAL PALM backs into Chattanooga in September 1963. The daily Cincinnati-Jacksonville ROYAL PALM was born in 1950 as the winter season-only NEW ROYAL PALM. In 1955, it became a year-round operation, and throughout the 1950s conveyed summer vacationers and winter-weary Midwesterners to Florida's sunny east coast. Now, the operation has obviously fallen from grace, and by 1970 the train that was once described as "tops" will be running as a one-car local through northern Kentucky. *(Walter E. Zullig photo)*

Above • Looking a little worse for the wear, Kansas City Southern E3 22 basks in the sunshine next to Alabama Great Southern F3A 6704 and an E7 mate at New Orleans in November 1963. A little history on these weary warriors: 6704 was delivered in November 1946. It was rebuilt to F7 specifications in 1951, and retired in 1972. KCS 22, meanwhile, began life in August 1939 as that road's two-spot for SOUTHERN BELLE service. In January 1942 she was renumbered 22. Still wearing that number, she went to scrap at Pittsburg, Kansas in 1964.

(Collection of Matt Herson)

Above • Here's another look at E6 2800, letting off a little steam at Birmingham Terminal Station in April 1964. Best guess is that 2800 and its mate are power for Train 18, the BIRMINGHAM SPECIAL. Check out that heavyweight Central of Georgia RPO a couple of tracks over.
(George Berisso photo)

Left • As a Cincinnati Union Terminal switcher toils in the background, a trio of Southern passenger F-units rolls through the yards at CUT in April 1964. In the Southern scheme of things, F-units numbered in the 6700 series were owned by subsidiary Alabama Great Southern, while the 4144 is an "original" Southern unit.
(Matt Herson photo)

Right • Pillows could be rented aboard Southern trains and came delivered in bags like this.
(Morning Sun Books Collection)

ABOVE • Frisco's October 1965 public timetable prominently featured the Kansas City-Birmingham sleeping car, which re-entered service following Frisco's 1965 passenger service restructuring. It was the last sleeper operated by the SLSF.
(Author's collection)

RIGHT • Birmingham Terminal Station at Fifth Avenue and 26th Street was home to a number of passenger roads, including Frisco, Illinois Central, Central of Georgia, Seaboard and Southern (Louisville & Nashville had its own depot at First Avenue and 20th Street South). Today, we're standing on the platform as the hand-off takes place between Frisco Train 105 and Southern Train 7, both carded as the KANSAS CITY-FLORIDA SPECIAL. Enjoy this scene while you can, because on this April 20, 1964, the combined operation is on borrowed time. In another month the Kansas City-Jacksonville sleeper will be eliminated by the Frisco (only to return briefly a short time later), and the train itself will follow in 1965. After that, Frisco will still run into Birmingham, but the only connections will be across the platform.
(George Berisso photo)

Above • The photographer didn't catch the name, but shake hands with the engineer in charge of FP7 6135 and mate 6133 as they take on fuel and water at Birmingham Terminal Station in July 1964. The train is No. 42, the northbound Pelican. She's due out at 7:30 AM, bound for Washington and connections beyond to New York City. *(Jim Thorington photo)*

Below • E6 2902 leads the way as the Pelican coasts through Greeneville, Tennessee on a murky morning in July 1964. The train's principal mission, totin, the mail, makes it anything but a speed merchant on its 212-mile run through Tennessee. Between Bristol and Chattanooga, Number 41 is scheduled for no fewer than 16 positive and conditional stops. By this time, though, the Pelican is undergoing extensive cutbacks. The New York-New Orleans sleeper has been eliminated south of Chattanooga and the diner is a Norfolk & Western operation only. *(Gib Allbach collection)*

ABOVE • Of all the E-units rostered by Southern (and subsidiary Central of Georgia), no group was more plentiful than the 28 E7As built between 1946 and 1949. Number 2921, seen here at Atlanta's Terminal Station in August 1964, was the next-to-the-last built. Southern got its money's worth out of this unit. She was delivered in April 1949, rebuilt to E8 rating (2,250 horsepower, up from 2,000) in 1957 and finally returned to EMD as a trade in September 1968. *(Jim Thorington photo)*

BELOW • Just for fun! "Back in the day," when engine men and conductors personalized their locomotives and cabooses, Savannah & Atlanta Pacific 750 had this elaborately-decorated eagle and brass candlesticks applied atop her headlight and number plate. The little Alco, photographed in August 1964, now makes its home at the Southeast Railway Museum in Duluth, Georgia. *(Jim Thorington photo)*

LEFT, ABOVE • Southern subsidiary Central of Georgia owned exactly two EMD E8 diesels, and here they are. The location is Birmingham's 27th Street crossing (where a Southern freight is cooling its heels in the distance). The date is September 1964 and the train is the joint Illinois Central-Central of Georgia-Atlantic Coast Line SEMINOLE. Even in the mid-1960s, this is still a pretty good train: sleepers and coaches from Chicago, with a St. Louis connection at Carbondale, and a Chicago-Columbus (Georgia) diner lounge. On the IC and Central of Georgia, she's Trains 9-10; on the ACL, she's 17-18. *(Jim Thorington photo)*

LEFT, BELOW • E6 2901 leads the BIRMINGHAM SPECIAL through the 27th Street crossing minutes away from arrival at Birmingham Terminal Station. Never a first-string passenger service, and down to coaches only on the south end of its Washington-New Orleans run, the SPECIAL by this date was surviving largely on the strength of its mail contract. Old car buffs will note the photographer's snappy-looking 1963 Dodge Dart in the lower right. *(Jim Thorington photo)*

ABOVE • Frisco named its E7 and E8 locomotives for famous race horses and military mounts. Here red-and-gold E8 2016 *Citation*, looking very much in need of a good scrubbing (and maybe a touchup as well), shares the platform with E8s on the point of Central of Georgia's SEMINOLE at Birmingham in the summer of 1964.

(Jim Thorington photo)

BELOW • Heavyweight coach 1042 brings up the markers of the Chattanooga-Memphis local as it calls at Decatur, Alabama in September 1964. Trains 35-36 operated across northern Alabama on a daylight schedule essentially opposite the better-patronized overnighter TENNESSEAN, and provided a cross-state connection for Southern Trains 17-18, the BIRMINGHAM SPECIAL. *(Bernie Wooler photo)*

LEFT, ABOVE • Well, we've seen Central of Georgia E8s masquerading in Illinois Central chocolate and orange. Now here's a look at the genuine article. IC 4040 takes a breather at the engine terminal in Birmingham during the summer of 1964. Later on, after a trip through the wash rack, she'll head back north as power for either the SEMINOLE or the CITY OF MIAMI. *(Jim Thorington photo)*

LEFT, BELOW • For a long season, the CRESCENT was the pride of Southern's passenger fleet, but by the mid-1960s, things had changed. These days, it's the SOUTHERNER that's the apple of management's eye, as evidenced by the glossy condition of E8 2929 leading the stainless consist into Birmingham. Between Atlanta and Birmingham, No. 47 is scheduled for only a single stop, at Anniston, Alabama. By the way, 2929 was the last E8 purchased by Southern. It survived into the Amtrak era, during which time it was renumbered 6916 and given a new coat of Virginia green paint. *(Jim Thorington photo)*

ABOVE • Bound for Memphis, mail and express Train 35 rolls through Huntsville, Alabama in November 1964. A caution here: Those seeking speedy transportation between Chattanooga and Memphis are advised to find alternate means. To cover the 270-odd mile route, No. 35 takes nine hours and five minutes and makes no fewer than 45 stops. On the other hand, is there a better way to see the rural south up close?
(Bernie Wooler photo)

BELOW • The ashcat leans out his window, as if measuring E8 6910 for a parking space at the mall. We're about 6 miles east of Birmingham, approaching Norris Yard in this November 1964 view. The E8 is a New Orleans & North Eastern unit, delivered in December 1953. The train is the Chattanooga-bound BIRMINGHAM SPECIAL, running with a single E-unit over the relatively flat terrain of northern Alabama.
(Jim Thorington photo)

Above • It's hard to know where to focus our attention for this shot, so let's take things in order. From left to right, we're looking at a 1963 Old F-85, followed by a 1962 or 1963 Ford Falcon, a 1956 Buick wagon and a 1964 Chevy. Oh, that big green job in the background is office car *Carolina*. She's a little older than the Detroit iron in the foreground, having rolled out of Pullman's shops in 1928. The car was rebuilt in 1963 and emerged with four master bedrooms and a sleeping compartment for the car attendant. Out of sight is car *Virginia*, to which the *Carolina* is permanently coupled. *(Jim Thorington photo)*

Above • It's a cloudy morning in Huntsville as Alabama Great Southern F7 6718 and an E7 mate lead local Train 35 past the depot. The train left Chattanooga at 8:00 AM (Eastern Time), and if it's on time won't get to Memphis until 4:10 PM. *(Bernie Wooller photo)*

ABOVE • Still in Huntsville, and at least the weather, if not the train-watching is better. It's August 1965 and Chattanooga-bound Train 36 is making its scheduled stop. From the look of that head end-heavy consist and Coolidge-era chair car, it's pretty clear that the primary business of this train is mail. *(Bernie Wooller photo)*

ABOVE • We're at Decatur, Alabama looking down at CNO&TP FP7 6146 on the point of a passenger train as it crosses the single track span over Joe Wheeler Lake. The lake, the largest in north Alabama, and the 72-foot high, 1.2 mile long dam that forms it are named for Confederate Cavalry Major General "Fightin," Joe Wheeler. This is the same Joe Wheeler who also served as the namesake for one of Southern's original two-car lightweight trains that entered service in 1939.

(Bernie Wooller photo)

ABOVE • With an unaccustomed face full of snow, Seaboard E8 3058 heads out of Birmingham toward Atlanta on a frigid day in February 1965. The train is No. 6-8, the morning all-stops local between Birmingham and Washington. In the consist this day are a duo of express boxes, a heavyweight baggage-RPO, an SAL lightweight coach, a Pennsy lightweight coach and a Seaboard heavyweight coach bringing up the markers. *(Jim Thorington photo)*

ABOVE • Central of Georgia E-units wore a number of liveries, including the original B&O-like blue and gray, the IC's brown and orange, and eventually the black/white/gold of parent Southern. Here's E7 808 paired with 803 at Birmingham in June 1965. Check the mounting of 808's bell. Was this unit unique? *(Jim Thorington photo)*

ABOVE • The CAROLINA SPECIAL was always a complex operation, and even by the July 23, 1965 date of this photo, such was still the case. Through its through cars have been eliminated, Nos. 27-28 still advertise PRR, NYC, B&O and C&O connections at Cincinnati for Chicago, Detroit and St. Louis. The SPECIAL is a combined train (with the PONCE DE LEON) Between Cincinnati and Oakdale, Tennessee, where it splits off for Asheville. There, the train separates a second time, with a "South Carolina Train" headed for Columbia and a "North Carolina Train" bound for Greensboro. Here, we're looking at the combined northbound train at Asheville. Power on this day is venerable (1947) Alabama Great Southern F3 6707. Looks like a little urban renewal is taking place at the left! *(Al Holtz photo)*

ABOVE • It's June 1966 in this photo and the deterioration of the area around Birmingham Terminal Station is complete. At the time of its grand opening on April 6, 1909, the Byzantine-style structure was hailed as a "Temple of Travel," and, for a time was served by an underground extension of the city's streetcar system. In 1926, an electric sign reading "Welcome to Birmingham, The Magic City" was erected (later, the "Welcome To" was deleted), and in 1940, a portion of the site was occupied by a federally-subsidized housing project. Fifty-four trains called daily in 1947, and 26 as late as 1960. However, in 1961, plans were being laid for reclaiming the site, sealing the station's doom. On September 21, 1969, the last CITY OF MIAMI called and the very next day the Burgin Demolition Company began taking the building down. In the scene above, the sign, the subway, the landscaping, everything but the building itself is already gone, and the wrecker's ball is right around the corner. *(Jim Thorington photo)*

ABOVE • Frisco had a reputation for good maintenance of its equipment, but apparently where locomotives were concerned, that did not extend to more than occasional trips through the wash rack. Grubby E8 2011, the former *Gallant Fox* and an E7 mate (yes, that's an E7 despite the E8 styling cues; look closely at the roof line) back down to their train at Birmingham on February 6, 1965. At 12:05 PM they'll be on their way to Kansas City with No. 106, the KANSAS CITY-FLORIDA SPECIAL.

(Gordon Lloyd photo, collection of Louis A. Marre)

ABOVE • There's plenty of power for this two-car job, seen here in September 1965. As the fireman climbs down from the cab, Train 35 arrives at Huntsville behind Alabama Great Southern F3A 6704 and a companion unit. Trailing are a heavyweight RPO and a single modernized coach. Despite the short consist, it's a safe bet there's plenty of room for those two youngsters waiting on the platform. However, the way passenger traffic is slipping, it's just as likely these two are just killing a little time doing some train-watching. *(Bernie Wooller photo)*

ABOVE • The caption written on the slide mount reads "Headed into Southern station Chattanooga, 4:30 PM, October 9, 1965." If that's the case, then this is Train 41, the Washington-New Orleans PELICAN, due in at 5:30 PM (the late Bernie Wooller, based in western Alabama, obviously had his watch set for Central Time). At this point in its run, No. 41's consist includes a Washington-New Orleans coach and a New York-Chattanooga 14-4 sleeper. Beyond Chattanooga, however, the PELICAN is coach only, and New Orleans is still 14 hours away!

(Bernie Wooller photo)

ABOVE • Southern's impressive station in Chattanooga as it appeared in the fall of 1965. Following the end of passenger service, the station was converted to a hotel and restaurant complex (the "Choo-Choo Hilton"), which featured sleeping rooms in retired railroad cars as well as a huge model railroad that included a floor-to-ceiling representation of nearby Lookout Mountain. *(Bernie Wooler photo)*

RIGHT • We're looking at a 1965 National Railway Historical Society fan trip, which should be apparent given the long string of heavyweight passenger-carrying cars, the steam generator car and the two freight units trailing passenger FP7 6141. *(Dave Ingles photo, collection of Matt Herson)*

BELOW • No caption information accompanied this photo, so let's see what we can figure out. The catenary above the tracks on the upper level makes it a safe bet we're in the Washington, D. C. area. The number of heavyweight cars in the consist tells us we're probably not looking at either the CRESCENT or the SOUTHERNER, and the fact that it's daylight pretty well eliminates the PIEDMONT in both directions, the PEACH QUEEN, the southbound PELICAN or the northbound TENNESSEAN. Best guess, based on the November 1965 date on the slide and the low light is that we're looking at Train 17, the BIRMINGHAM SPECIAL, due out of Washington Union Station at 3:50 PM. Fair enough?

(Emery Gulash, Morning Sun Books Collection)

LEFT • Another look at the fan trip, this time from the inside out. Even though Southern went to some length to upgrade their aging heavyweight equipment, there is still no mistaking the 1920s vintage of this day coach. That said, if all of Southern's passenger trains were as well-patronized as this one, perhaps President Brosnan would have taken a less aggressive approach to pruning the company's varnish during the 1960s.

(Lawson Hill photo, collection of Boston Chapter, NRHS)

If it's fall in Tennessee, it's got to be time for Volunteer football. In this December 5, 1965 view at Knoxville, we're looking at Extra 6911 powering a trainload of football fans heading home after a 27-24 win over Memphis State the previous afternoon. For fans of Tennessee football, the Vols went 7 wins, 1 loss, 2 ties during the 1965 season, and defeated Tulsa 27-6 in that year's Bluebonnet Bowl.
(Dave Ingles photo, collection of Matt Herson)

Above • E7 2909 and a passenger F-unit power Train 35, the daytime Chattanooga-Memphis local as it departs Huntsville, Alabama in December 1965. The line peeling off to the right is the fourteen-mile branch to Hobbs Island. *(Bernie Wooller photo)*

Below • There isn't too much to say about this photo, taken at Huntsville in February 1966, except that it seems incongrous to see such a cold scene this far south. Looking more like the "Polar Express" than a Southern local, E7 2921 leads a mate on the point of the Chattanooga-Memphis day train. *(Bernie Wooller photo)*

ABOVE • An A-B-A set of E-units leads Train 48, the SOUTHERNER, through Alexandria, Virginia on a frigid February 26, 1966. On the point this day is E8 6908, a NO&NE unit delivered in December 1953. By this date, we're looking at what is unquestionably Southern's best train, as included in the consist are no fewer than five lightweight sleepers, a tavern-lounge, coaches and a dining car open all the way from Washington to New Orleans. North of Washington, the SOUTHERNER's through cars will be in the consist of Pennsylvania Train 148, the combined SOUTHERNER/SILVER COMET.

(George Menge photo, collection of Matt Herson)

ABOVE • Alabama Great Southern 6706 and mate SR 4138 await their next assignment alongside the platform at Cincinnati Union Terminal on an overcast April 23, 1966. Both units are F3s, acquired in 1946 and 1947 respectively. The units had relatively long careers, each toiling for 26 years before reaching retirement in the early 1970s.

(Emery Gulash photo, Morning Sun Books Collection)

ABOVE • It's a little later in the day and the F-units have got a roll on Train 3-41, the ROYAL PALM (with a Birmingham-New Orleans connection via the PELICAN). The PALM is a far cry from the streamliner of the 1950s that featured coaches and sleepers from as far away as Chicago, Detroit and Cleveland. Today's train is a coach-plus-coach-lounge job that operates between the Queen City and the Georgia metropolis of Valdosta, just north of the Georgia-Florida state line. During the 1960s, Southern was notorious for truncating its trains just outside major terminals as a way of discouraging riders. From the abbreviated consist of today's No. 3, the tactic is obviously having an effect.
(Emery Gulash photo, Morning Sun Books Collection)

ABOVE • We're back in Huntsville, watching the station stop of the Chattanooga-Memphis local as it boards passengers and mail in the spring of 1966. Looking over the consist that trails this day's pair of F-units, not a single passenger-carrying car is in sight! *(Bernie Wooller photo)*

ABOVE • Here's the real business of just about every Southern passenger train during the 1960s except the CRESCENT and the SOUTHERNER. Lightweight car 1727 was built by ACF in 1950 as a baggage-mail with a 60-foot postal apartment. Number 1727 and sisters SR 1728 and CNO&TP remained on the roster until 1979, when Southern's privately-operated passenger service ceased for good. *(Bernie Wooller photo)*

ABOVE • A Cincinnati Union Terminal switcher busies itself with a long cut of mail and express cars, including a pair of colorful Chesapeake & Ohio heavyweights as a Southern passenger train threads its way through the complex CUT trackage. Judging from the train's length, this is likely the combined CAROLINA SPECIAL/PONCE DE LEON, with traffic from Columbia, Asheville and (you got it), Valdosta, Georgia. Not long after this photo was made, the PONCE DE LEON's route was trimmed back again, this time to a more sensible Cincinnati-Atlanta run. *(Emery Gulash photo, Morning Sun Books Collection)*

ABOVE • Looking from the angle of the photo like its moving a mile-a-minute (but actually standing still), Train No. 3, the ROYAL PALM, calls at Lexington, Kentucky in May 1966. The timetable calls for a ten-minute dwell time in the Kentucky capitol city, more than long enough to board the few passengers who are riding the former Florida flagship these days. *(Tom Smart photo, collection of Matt Herson)*

ABOVE • It's amazing the people who turn out for railroad fan trips. In July 1966, no less than Southern Railway Vice President of Law W. Graham Claytor snaps a photo of SR business car No. 3 bringing up the markers of a National Railway Historical Society (Atlanta Chapter) excursion train. Fan trip or not, however, there were no "casual days" on the Southern, as the president-in-waiting is wearing a dark business suit. His boss, Mr. D. W. Brosnan, wouldn't have it any other way!

(Jim Thorington photo)

ABOVE • Southern passenger units swap war stories at the terminal in Birmingham, Alabama, as they await their next assignments in August 1966. Keeping one another company are FP7 6144 and E6 units 2900 and 2902. During this period, SR trains calling at Birmingham included the PELICAN, BIRMINGHAM SPECIAL and SOUTHERNER, plus Trains 7-8, the connecting train for Frisco's SOUTHLAND. *(Jim Thorington photo)*

BELOW • The high-ceilinged waiting room at Southern's depot in Huntsville provides a look at standard passenger railroading late in the classic era. Note the wooden benches, hanging light fixtures, dark-stained wainscoting and cove moldings. The ticket window looks dark, though, so we may be in for a wait before the next train.

(Bernie Wooller photo)

Above • What does a mail train look like after the mail is gone? Well, in a word, this. Beginning in the mid-1960s, Southern undertook an aggressive campaign to consolidate its trains across Tennessee. The passenger business had gone into severe decline, and the remaining mail could easily be accommodated by the reasonably well-patronized Tennessean. The result was that daylight locals 35-36 found themselves without meaningful work to do, as evidenced by the sadly diminished two-car job seen here at Huntsville in February 1967. The train is on borrowed time, and will be gone in a matter of days. *(Bernie Wooller photo)*

Right • Following the death of local Trains 35-36, the Arrivals & Departures board at Huntsville now shows a single schedule, the Washington-Memphis Tennessean. Of course, by the date of this photo in February 1967, the Tennessean is itself little more than a local operation. Betwen Memphis and Chattanooga, Nos. 45-46 are coach-only, plus a cut of head end of equipment. North of Chattanooga, though, things look up a bit, as the train adds a pair of sleepers and a N&W-operated diner-lounge between Bristol and Roanoke.
(Bernie Wooller photo)

Below • Freight F3 4149 shares the afternoon sunshine at Ivy City with E7 2916 and a mate on February 26, 1967. The catenary wires in the background carry the juice for Pennsy's legendary GG1s, which handle the Keystone Road's freight and passenger trains between Washington and New York City.
(George Berisso photo)

ABOVE • Well-documented is the fall from grace during the late 1950s and early 1960s of Southern's ROYAL PALM, as it deteriorated from a fourteen-car streamliner to a coach job incongruously terminating in south Georgia. Well, check out the competition. Here's Louisville & Nashville Train 18, the northbound FLAMINGO, itself a former Florida flyer, making its nightly stop at Knoxville with a consist that includes a string of head-end cars and a single coach. Say what you will about railroads abandoning the traveling public, but between Southern and L&N it looks very much like it was the public that gave up first.

(Lyle Key photo)

ABOVE • Must be a lot colder than it looks! Despite a generous helping of southern sunshine, there's plenty of ice clinging to F3 4138 and a companion FP7 as they lead Train 2, the northbound PONCE DE LEON through Louisville on February 26, 1967. No, the PONCE hasn't exchanged its northern terminus from Ohio to Kentucky. However, today there's a wreck on the Rathole Division, and the PONCE is taking the long way around. *(Tom Smart photo, collection of Matt Herson)*

In terms of Florida railroading, Jacksonville Terminal Station was where the action was. Trains from as far away as St. Louis, Kansas City, Chicago, Detroit, New York and Boston all funneled through cars and through passengers into Jacksonville, where they were forwarded by Florida East Coast, Seaboard and Atlantic Coast Line for resort towns such as Miami, Ft. Lauderdale, Palm Beach and Tampa-St. Pete. In this view, power from SAL, ACL, L&N and FEC (look closely for this one!) soak up a little warmth on a sunny February 25, 1967. By this time, FEC, which had toughed out a strike by its operating crafts, was down to a single schedule between Jacksonville and North Miami. *(George Berisso photo)*

Above • Sailing along under PRR catenary at Washington is D.C.-Atlanta mail and express Train 21. Like mail trains on many roads, No. 21 did not appear in public timetables of the period and, although it was scheduled as a first-class train, it did not solicit passengers. It was, however, an early "intermodal" train, and usually picked up a string of piggyback cars just south of Alexandria. The flats did not accompany the train through the Capitol Hill Tunnel and into Washington Union Station. *(George H. Menge photo, collection of Matt Herson)*

Above • Spring is in the air as Train 17, the southbound BIRMINGHAM SPECIAL rounds a curve at Burke, Virginia, on a balmy April 2, 1967. Burke is located 11.7 miles south of Alexandria, and is not a stop for any of Southern's passenger trains except for northbound mail train 36, which can be flagged as the train passes through at 5:07 A. M. *(Al Holtz photo)*

ABOVE • Just underway on its 803.3 mile run to its namesake city, Southern Train 17, the BIRMINGHAM SPECIAL rumbles through Alexandria, Virginia. E7 2906 trails what appears to be an endless string of express cars, and it takes a sharp eye to spot the rider cars buried deep in the consist. Never a train that handled many streamlined cars, the SPECIAL on this Saturday, June 10, 1967, is down to coaches only over the entire length of its run. *(Al Holtz photo)*

BELOW • Sleeper *Piedmont Valley* is one of six 14-4 cars built by Pullman-Standard in November 1949 for general passenger service. So far, so good, but what's it doing in St. Louis, bring up the markers of what is apparently a Frisco passenger train? Frisco-Southern through-car operations in and out of St. Louis ended years before, and by the September 1967 date of this photo, Frisco no longer offered sleeping car service on its single train between St. Louis and Oklahoma City. A special movement, perhaps? *(Paul C. Winters photo)*

A Richmond, Fredericksburg & Potomac E8 leads Seaboard Coast Line's SILVER COMET into Alexandria's colonial-style depot on a crystal-clear day in August 1967. The COMET was Southern's primary competitor between Washington and Birmingham, and for a season was a pretty good train. The train, however, was not a one-railroad operation. Between Richmond and Washington, it ran over the rails of the RF&P, as did every other SCL passenger train.
(Paul Coe photo)

ABOVE • E7s 2915, 2908 and Alabama Great Southern F2 6701 roll slowly past the engine terminal at Ivy City in Washington, D. C. in October 1967. That F2 is a rare bird; only four of them were acquired by the Southern system, and only 60 were purchased by U. S. railroads altogether. As built, F2s produced 1,350 horsepower (like the earlier FTs), and bridged the gap between the FT and the subsequent 1,500 horsepower F3. Number 6701 was built in July 1946, upgraded in 1951 to F7 rating, and remained on the roster for 26 years.
(W. J. Brennan photo, Morning Sun Books Collection)

ABOVE • We're in Atlanta, looking down at the complex track work leading into Terminal Station as E6 2902 rolls past the camera in August 1967. Take a long, last look at this fancy filly, as retirement is only days away. She'll be returned to EMD as a trade-in the very next month, after a career that spanned better than twenty-six years. *(Morning Sun Books Collection)*

RIDING THE CAROLINA SPECIAL

The CAROLINA SPECIAL traced its origin to the year 1911, when it began operations between Cincinnati and Charleston by way of Knoxville and Asheville. In 1923, it was expanded into two sections, a "North Carolina Train" and a "South Carolina Train," with Asheville as the junction point. The North Carolina section ran between Asheville and Goldsboro, while the main stem of the train continued to operate into Charleston. In the period following World War II, the train often ran with as many as seven sleepers, and enjoyed considerable military traffic. However, after the Korean War, passenger volume went into decline, and by 1958, the SPECIAL and the PONCE DE LEON were combined between Cincinnati and Oakdale, Tennessee. In 1962, service between Columbia and Charleston was discontinued, and the following year through service to Chicago also ended. In 1967, the North Carolina section was combined with the ASHEVILLE SPECIAL and ran only between Salisbury and Asheville (interestingly, this stub operation would survive until 1975). The remnant of the South Carolina section operated only a short time longer, making its final run on December 6, 1968. In the spring of that year, however, noted Chicago-based rail photographer and historian Jim Neubauer rode the "South Carolina" section of the CAROLINA SPECIAL from Tryon to Cincinnati. Thanks to the outstanding photos he took along the way, we can come along for the ride nearly forty years later. *(All photos by Jim Neubauer)*

ABOVE • Here's the depot at Tryon, where Jim boarded for the northbound run of Train 27-2, the CAROLINA SPECIAL.

ABOVE • The train rolls into Tryon on the advertised, with a diminutive consist headed by F3 4144. This unit was not originally delivered with a steam boiler, but in a reversal of the usual course of events received the upgrade during shopping at Chattanooga in 1949.
LEFT • The next stop en route is Saluda, and its fearsome 4.7% mainline grade. Here, Jim has grabbed a shot from the rear vestibule of the single heavyweight coach that makes up the entire passenger carrying portion of the train south of Asheville.
RIGHT • The SPECIAL departs Saluda, bound for Tuxedo, Flat Rock Hendersonville and points north to Asheville.

Above • The SPECIAL has arrived at Asheville. We'll have some time here to hit the platform and stretch our legs while a switch crew tacks on a 10-6 lightweight sleeper bound for Cincinnati. For those who might want a bite to eat, there are vending machines inside offering soft drinks and Tom's Snacks, a brand familiar throughout the South.

Left • The Asheville-Cincinnati sleeper, a Pullman-Standard *River*-series 10-6 Pullman, has been tacked onto the rear of the train.

Below • With the consist buttoned up, Number 27 is ready to go. A tug on the conductor's communication line and we're on our way.

Left • Running north and west along the French Broad River. For obvious reasons, the location was a favorite spot for photographers to stalk both freight and passenger trains. Can any railroad boast a prettier line?

ABOVE • Judging from the spanking-clean condition of E8 6911 and mates, one is tempted to speculate that this must be the SOUTHERNER or the CRESCENT, since by this May 1968 date, these were the only Southern passenger trains one could be sure would still be looking sharp. However, the caption accompanying this view indicates we're in Louisville, Kentucky. That makes this either a detour or a special movement. Best guess, given the date and the condition of Southern's Cincinnati trains, it's power for a Kentucky Derby Special, long a tradition of railroads serving the South. Oh, yes--the winner of the 94th Run for the Roses was *Forward Pass*, in 2:02-1/5. Did you have a bet down? *(Tom Smart photo, collection of Matt Herson)*

ABOVE • Here's E7 2919 on another day as it leads Train No. 3, the southbound ROYAL PALM out of town at Cincinnati in July 1968. Despite the train's "end is near" appearance, the PALM would hang on for another year and a half before bowing out for good in January 1970. By that time, she was only running as far south as Somerset, Kentucky. *(Collection of Gib Allbach)*

Above • Chances are that if FP7 6133 sits at the old depot in Asheville too much longer, it'll get swallowed up by that kudzu running wild in the background. As it is, the indestructible weed has climbed halfway up that line pole, and if somebody doesn't cut it back, it'll grow right down those communication lines! *(Collection of Gib Allbach)*

Above • Trailing a Railway Express reefer and a string of express cars behind freshly-scrubbed E8 6909, Royal Palm No. 3 pays a call at Lexington, Kentucky on a sunny morning in July 1968. Delivered in December 1953, 6909 would turn out to be a real survivor, lasting into the post-Amtrak Southern Crescent era and named George Wythe in honor of the nation's Bicentennial. celebration Following the end of Southern passenger service, the unit was sold to rebuilder Precision National Corporation in November 1979, concluding a run just short of 26 years. *(Mac Owen photo, collection of Bob Wilt)*

LEFT, ABOVE • The only serious competition Southern faced between Washington and Atlanta was from the Seaboard Air Line, which fielded a highly successful fleet of streamliners in its own right between the nation's capital and the southeast. Despite being known principally for its Florida trains, Seaboard (and successor Seaboard Coast Line) did offer a pretty good train in Nos. 33-34, the New York-Birmingham SILVER COMET, seen here behind SCL power at Atlanta Terminal Station in July 1968. Despite being an also-ran compared to Southern's CRESCENT and SOUTHERNER, the COMET did offer a 10-6 sleeper and a tavern-coach over the length of its run. *(Paul Coe photo)*

LEFT, BELOW • We're at Biltmore, North Carolina, watching Southern's ASHEVILLE SPECIAL loading passengers on August 1, 1969. Biltmore is five miles and five minutes from Asheville, and is the junction point for the Charleston and Goldsboro lines. Amazingly, given the minuscule consist of this day's train, the SPECIAL ended up surviving into the Amtrak era to become a tourist favorite that most days included in its consist an ex-Wabash CITY OF ST. LOUIS dome-coach. *(Doug Nuckles photo)*

RIGHT • For some reason, Southern's summer 1969 timetable had artwork that featured what appear to be EMD FTs. Compare the relatively austere appearance of this version with the 1963 timetable that appears previously. Clearly, the bloom is off the rose!

BELOW • Another look at the ASHEVILLE SPECIAL, this time at the depot in Asheville. Sharp-eyed observers will note that a switcher is working at the rear of the train. F-unit 6707 is an Alabama Great Southern F3, delivered in 1947, equipped with a steam generator in 1949 and upgraded to F7 rating in 1950. Number 6707 enjoyed a career of 26 years, with the curtain finally falling in 1973 when she was returned to EMD as a trade-in. *(Doug Nuckles photo)*

On August 19, 1969, Hurricane Camille made landfall at Pass Christian, Mississippi, packing winds of 200 mph and dumping torrents of rain up and down the east coast. In the process, Southern's Charlottesville-Lynchburg main line was shut down for better than a week. As a result, Southern trains, including the premiere SOUTHERNER were forced to detour via Richmond, and then over the Richmond, Fredericksburg & Potomac into Washington. Here's Number 48 at RF&Ps Acca Yard at 11:20 AM on August 31, 1969 behind four E8s. She's due into Washington at 9:15, which puts her just about three hours late at this point. *(Doug Nuckles photo)*

ABOVE • Residents and railfans of Richmond alike got a rare visit from Southern's passenger fleet thanks to Hurricane Camille. This time we're looking at Train 18, the BIRMINGHAM SPECIAL rolling north at Bassett Avenue and powered by five F-units, including F3 4145 on the point. *(Doug Nuckles photo)*

BELOW • In 1963, welterweight Central of Georgia was merged into the Southern system, adding 10 E7s to the SR roster (E8s 811 and 812 were also part of the package, but retained their chocolate and orange IC-like paint for joint SEMINOLE and CITY OF MIAMI service). In this view, dating from August 24, 1969, E7 805 catches a little sunshine at Atlanta's Terminal Station. 805 began life in 1946 and remained in service until 1970, when it was returned to EMD for trade-in credit. *(Collection of Gib Allbach)*

Above • Southern Train No. 3, the three-car ROYAL PALM is due of out Cincinnati at 8:45 AM, bound for Atlanta (the Jacksonville terminus was eliminated in 1966). Today, the consist is a single 522-series heavyweight express car and a couple of coaches behind surprisingly glossy E8 6914. In the background can be seen the palisades overlooking the Ohio River at Covington, on the Kentucky side. *(R. J. Yanosey photo)*

Above • Trains bound for Cincinnati Union Terminal from the south crossed into the Queen City over the Ohio River Bridge, between Cincinnati and Ludlow, Kentucky. The Bridge, in turn, was accessed by a system of ramps, which provided an excellent location for photographers intent on capturing an "aerial" shot of arriving and departing trains. In this October 12, 1969 view, Train No. 3 threads its way out of town with a four-car consist behind E7 2814.

(Collection of Gib Allbach)

Above • Another look at the former Royal Palm, rumbling out of Cincinnati over the high bridge on a dreary morning in October 1966. This morning's consist includes a baggage-express heavyweight, a pair of lightweight coaches and E7 2916 *(Jim Neubauer photo)*

Above • In September 1969, Englishman Alan Pegler brought ex-London & North Eastern Railway 4-6-2 No. 4472, the *Flying Scotsman*, to the United States for a 2200-mile tour between Boston and Houston, Texas. Included in the consist were two tenders (one a "canteen" car) and nine coaches containing exhibits of various products manufactured in England. The 4-6-2 was purchased by Pegler in 1963 for $7,200, who then spent another $91,200 of his own money on her renovation. Here, fitted with an American-style pilot, bell, whistle and coupler, the *Flying Scotsman* is seen in a stunning night shot at Atlanta's Terminal Station in November 1969. *(Emery Gulash photo, Morning Sun Books Collection)*

Left • During her tour of the United States, the *Flying Scotsman* ran over the Southern rails between Washington and Meridian, Mississippi. Never one to pass on an opportunity to generate positive public relations, Southern President Graham Claytor arranged for a meet among L&NE 4472 and Southern steam engines 750 and 4501 at Anniston, Alabama. The event commemorated not only the visit of the *Flying Scotsman*, but also the 75th birthday of Southern and the 150th birthday of the state of Alabama. In this photo, 4472 owner Alan Pegler beams at the camera while SR President Claytor addresses the crowd assembled for the occasion.

(Emery Gulash photo, Morning Sun Books Collection)

Above • The caption information accompanying this photo reads as follows: "Terminal Station in Birmingham the last month it was in service. Demolition has already commenced on the mail and baggage sections flanking the main section pictured. A small brick station at the rear has almost been completed to handle the three remaining trains (Southern, Central of Georgia, Illinois Central)." So, what else is there to add? Oh, yes. The photo is dated Monday, November 3, 1969. *(Al Holtz photo)*

Right, Above and Below • We're looking at Union Station in Atlanta in November, 1969. The front view is a revealing vignette of what folks were driving in 1969, including three Volkswagen Beetles, three Chevrolet Corvairs and a Renault Dauphine (!), all of which were powered by air-cooled rear engines. In the back can be seen the system of covered stairways leading to the tracks below street level. Union Station served passenger trains of Louisville & Nashville (note the billboard in the background) and pre-merger Nashville, Chattanooga & St. Louis.

Nearby Terminal Station was home to Southern, Atlanta & West Point, Seaboard and pre-merger Central of Georgia. Union Station continued to host passenger trains right up until Amtrak startup day on May 1, 1971, when L&N's local train from St. Louis was discontinued. Union Station was demolished later that year as part of a major downtown renewal project.

(Both Emery Gulash, Morning Sun Books Collection)

Enjoy Luxurious Streamliner Travel Comfort between NEW YORK and NEW ORLEANS (via Washington, Atlanta and Birmingham) Take The Southerner

Above • TR2 switch engine 2403 idles at Atlanta Terminal Station, awaiting its next chore, on a wet afternoon in November 1969. Opened in 1905, Terminal Station saw daily passenger totals in excess of 30,000 during World War II. Terminal Station served as host to Southern's varnish until June 14, 1970, when it was closed and SR moved its passenger operations to suburban Peachtree Station northeast of downtown (subsidiary Central of Georgia moved its only Atlanta train, the NANCY HANKS II to Spring Street Station). Terminal Station fell to the wrecker's ball in 1972 to make room for a new federal office complex.
(Emery Gulash photo, Morning Sun Books Collection)

Above • In 1910, a statue of Samuel Spencer, "Father of the Southern Railway System" was erected in front of Terminal Station with funds contributed by the railroad's employees. Following the demolition of Terminal Station, the statue was relocated to the grounds of Peachtree Station in north suburban Atlanta. However, in 1996 the statue was returned to its original downtown location (and its original pedestal mount) as part of the city's Olympic renovations.
(Emery Gulash photo, Morning Sun Books Collection)

Above • A lone lineside observer waves at the crew of Southern Mikado 4501 near Anniston, Alabama in November 1969. The Mike, along with London & North Eastern 4-6-2 4472 were on the last leg of an Atlanta-Birmingham run. For the occasion, 4501, a 1911 product of the Baldwin Locomotive Works, is sporting an auxiliary 18-ton, 20,000 gallon ex-Central of Georgia "canteen" tender, this to extend her range between water stops. Rescued from a sure date with the scrapper by a private individual named Paul Merriman, 4501 became the first Southern freight steam locomotive to wear the venerated green livery.

(Doug Nuckles photo)

Above • So much caption information accompanied this slide, it's hard to know where to start. It's 9:21 AM Tuesday, November 4, 1969 and we're at Attalla, Alabama, checking out the power for Southern Train 17, the Birmingham Special. Today's consist includes F7 4133 and FP7 6143, a modernized heavyweight combine, Norfolk & Western lightweight coach 1830 (originally a Wabash car) and two mail-storage cars, one from New York and one from Philadelphia. One more thing: at this point, No. 17 is running 26 minutes late! *(Al Holtz photo)*

ABOVE • Backed by mate 808, Central of Georgia E7 805 looks like she could use a bath as she heads up C of G Train 107, the NANCY HANKS II, at Macon, Georgia on December 14, 1969. Over its 290-mile run, the little streamliner offers a remarkable array of amenities, including lightweight coaches, an ex-Wabash BLUE BIRD dome-parlor car (which included a conference area called the "Saddle and Stirrup Room") and a grill-lounge serving light meals and beverages. Try finding anything like that on Southern proper. *(J. W. Swanberg photo)*

BELOW • Trains 3-4, the coach-only remnant of the ROYAL PALM are very much on borrowed time in this view at Somerset, Kentucky in January 1970. By this time, the Kentucky hamlet is the southern terminus of the train which once ran fourteen cars long between Cincinnati and Jacksonville, and offered connections from as far away as Detroit, Chicago and Cleveland. Last run for the sorry little train was only days ahead, on January 31. *(Collection of Gib Allbach)*

ABOVE • Alan Pegler's *Flying Scotsman* smokes it up on a London-like foggy morning in Birmingham in May 1970. For those curious about such things, 4472 was a three-cylinder locomotive fitted with 80-inch driving wheels and was the first locomotive in England to officially exceed 100 MPH. She was built in Doncaster in January 1923 and operated in regular service between London and Edinburgh, Scotland until her retirement and eventual purchase by Pegler. *(Jim Thorington photo)*

ABOVE • Here's a look at FP7 6149 at Ivy City in Washington. There's a small amount of history associated with this unit, as it was the last FP7 built for Southern. Sublettered for the CNO&TP, 6149 was delivered in December 1950, and remained on the roster an astonishing 29 years! *(Emery Gulash photo, Morning Sun Books Collection)*

ABOVE • We've got a little bit of everything in this photo, taken at Birmingham on April 22, 1970. On the left, an unidentified switch engine shuffles a short cut of heavyweight cars from the BIRMINGHAM SPECIAL. On the right, F3 4133 and an F7 mate face off with business car 23. That F3 is one of the oldest passenger locomotives on the roster, having entered service in November 1946. *(George Berisso photo)*

ABOVE • In February 1970, the SOUTHERNER officially gained recognition as the premiere train of the railroad, as the CRESCENT and the PEACH QUEEN were consolidated and renamed the PIEDMONT. The SOUTHERNER, meanwhile, was renumbered 1-2 and renamed the SOUTHERN CRESCENT. Here, flanked by Illinois Central power and rolling stock, the flagship idles at New Orleans on April 22, 1970. By this time, the SOUTHERN CRESCENT is the last SR passenger train serving the Big Easy, as the "new" PIEDMONT ran only as far as Atlanta.

(George Berisso photo)

Above • The TENNESSEAN, PELICAN and BIRMINGHAM SPECIAL were all operated jointly by Southern and Norfolk & Western. Thus, it was not uncommon to see N&W equipment in the consist of these trains anywhere along their routes between Washington and Memphis, Birmingham or New Orleans. In this 1970 photo, car 1733 lays over at Birmingham. This car was built in 1941 as a class Pm 60-seat coach for service in the premiere POCAHONTAS, between Norfolk and Columbus, Ohio. Originally delivered in N&W's Pennsy-like Tuscan red, it was repainted Wabash blue when N&W standardized on that color for its post-merger passenger trains. Car 1733 was sold to Canada's Ontario Northland in 1971. *(Jim Thornigton photo)*

Above • E8 2926 and a trio of mates await their next assignment at Ivy City in July 1970. Considering the 9,000 horsepower packed by this lashup, as well as their immaculately clean condition, it's a pretty safe bet these ladies are slated for duty on the flagship SOUTHERN CRESCENT, as by this late date no other Southern passenger train rated anything approaching this. *(R. J. Yanosey photo)*

ABOVE • Well now, here's some seniority! Double-slotted Southern steam power, including consolidation 722 on the point head up a National Railway Historical Society excursion train at Yemassee, South Carolina on Seaboard Coast Line rails in September 1970. Yemassee, by the way, is noteworthy in its own right as the jumping-off point for the United States Marine Corps. recruit depot and training station at Parris Island. *(Emery Gulash photo, Morning Sun Books Collection)*

ABOVE • Another look at 2-8-0 no. 722. This little jewel was originally built by Baldwin in 1904 and delivered as class Ks with 24" x 30" cylinders, 57" drivers and 46,700 pounds of tractive effort. She was later upgraded to class Ks-1 status and sold to the East Tennessee & Western North Carolina (the "Tweetsie") as their number 208. Southern later repurchased the engine, renumbered it back to 722 and painted in green and gold for excursion service.

(Emery Gulash photo, Morning Sun Books Collection)

Above • E8 6912 and three mates lead the Southern Crescent at Birmingham, Alabama on September 29, 1970. Looks like the train is handling some extra (possibly deadhead) equipment today, including a heavyweight baggage car, as the Crescent is normally a "pure" streamliner over the length of its run between Washington and New Orleans. *(Bob Wilt photo)*

Above • A switch engine escorts a brace of E8s at Southern's Peagram Shops on Atlanta's south side. Peagram was a usual service point for SR passenger power, including locomotives assigned to the flagship Southern Crescent. During the layover at Peachtree Station, incoming road power was swapped out for fresh horses. 2926, seen here in the trailing position, is a 1951 graduate of La Grange. Renumbered 6903 in 1972, she remained on the roster an additional seven years before being retired and sold to the New Jersey Department of Transportation for duty in New York-area commuter service.

(Morning Sun Books Collection)

SOUTHERN RAILWAY *Through* PASSENGER SERVICE
1971-1979: GOING OUT IN STYLE

Despite the cutbacks begun in the middle and late 1950s, Southern Railway at the beginning of the 1960s still operated a fairly impressive fleet of trains, principally on its main lines between Washington-New Orleans, Washington-Birmingham and Cincinnati-Jacksonville. In the fall of 1961, for example, travelers could find the following main line trains listed in Southern's timetable:

NUMBERS	TRAIN NAME	OPERATING BETWEEN
1-2	PONCE DE LEON	Cincinnati-Jacksonville
3-4	ROYAL PALM	Cincinnati-Jacksonville
7-8	KANSAS CITY-FLORIDA SPECIAL	Kansas City-Jacksonville
15-16	ASHEVILLE SPECIAL	Greensboro-Goldsboro
17-18	BIRMINGHAM SPECIAL	New York-Birmingham
21-22	CAROLINA SPECIAL (North)	Cincinnati-Goldsboro
27-28	CAROLINA SPECIAL (South)	Cincinnati-Asheville
29-30	PEACH QUEEN	New York-Atlanta
31-32	AUGUSTA SPECIAL	Charlotte-Augusta
33-34	PIEDMONT LIMITED	New York-New Orleans
35-36		Washington-New Orleans
37-38	CRESCENT	New York-New Orleans
41-42	PELICAN	New York-New Orleans
45-46	TENNESSEAN	Washington-Memphis
47-48	SOUTHERNER	New York-New Orleans

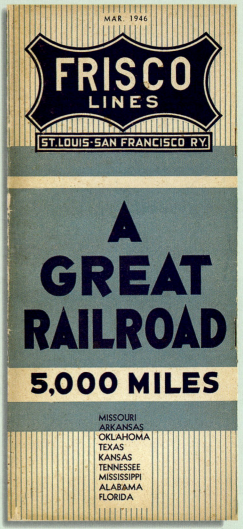

ABOVE • *In the 1940s, Frisco and Southern operated a number four trains daily between Florida and St. Louis and Kansas City.*
(Author's collection)

Without question, some of these trains were mere ghosts of their former selves, having lost their diners, sleepers and through cars to points beyond Jacksonville and Cincinnati. Others remained in reasonably good shape, and on the Southern in the early and middle 1960s, it was still possible for travelers to get to and from most of the same destinations they could have ridden twenty years before. As the 1960s unfolded, however, it became increasingly evident that the opportunity to ride Southern trains was not to last much longer. For example, despite President W. Graham Claytor's statement in 1968 that his railroad "wanted to stay in the passenger business," less than 2% of its gross the previous year came from transporting people. Indeed, in a follow-up interview two years later with *Railway Age*, Claytor summed up his company's current view of its passenger service:

"Like any other railroad in the passenger business, we have a passenger-train problem. The passenger service we operate is operated at the highest possible quality level. We think this is the only intelligent way. [However] most of the trains that we have been running serve no purposes except in the past to haul United States mail. What we have done, accordingly, is to discontinue these unused trains. I ... do not think there is likely to be a long-range future for the long-distance passenger train."

As in past years, the Pennsylvania Railroad continued to provide through-car service between Washington and New York for the CRESCENT, PELICAN, PIEDMONT, TENNESSEAN, SOUTHERNER, BIRMINGHAM SPECIAL and PEACH QUEEN. Through cars for the AUGUSTA SPECIAL and ASHEVILLE SPECIAL were handled by the CRESCENT between Washington-Charlotte and Washington-Greensboro, respectively. Across-the-platform connections for the ROYAL PALM were available in Cincinnati with the New York Central, Pennsylvania and Baltimore & Ohio for cities as distant as Chicago, Detroit, Cleveland and St. Louis. However, through-car service was no longer offered at the Queen City. The CRESCENT, however, still exchanged cars with the West Point Route at Atlanta.

Apart from Washington and Atlanta, the only other Southern through-car gateway in the 1960s was Birmingham. There, the Frisco, which originated the KANSAS CITY-FLORIDA SPECIAL in Kansas City, handed off coaches and a sleeper bound for Jacksonville.

In the late 1940s, the KANSAS CITY-FLORIDA SPECIAL operation included three heavyweight Kansas City-Jacksonville sleepers (one for the exclusive use of military personnel), plus coaches and a diner-lounge between Kaycee and Birmingham. By 1961, however, the SPECIAL was down to a pair of coaches and a single lightweight Frisco 14-4 sleeper between Kansas City and Jacksonville. Meal service was provided by a heavyweight Frisco diner-lounge that operated between Springfield, Missouri and Birmingham. Prior to 1960 the SPECIAL had also carried a 10-1-2 Kansas City-Birmingham sleeper, but this car was discontinued in 1959 due to low patronage.

East of Birmingham and on Southern rails, the SPECIAL dropped the Frisco diner and added a Southern coach and coach-diner. At Atlanta Terminal Station the coach-diner came off and an Atlanta-Brunswick, Georgia 10-section, 2-drawing room heavyweight sleeper was added. In 1961, however, meal service over the Southern portion of the run was eliminated, and passengers had to grab whatever refreshments they could during the layover at Birmingham. Sadly, this interesting operation did not survive beyond the middle of the decade.

In May 1964, Frisco eliminated the 14-4 sleeping car from its Nos. 105-106, temporarily ending Pullman service between Kansas City and the southeast. Sixteen months later, on September 17, 1965, Frisco discontinued the KANSAS CITY-FLORIDA SPECIAL outright as part of a system-wide "restructuring" of its passenger service. After that, Kansas City-Birmingham service was via Trains 101-102, the former SUNNYLAND, now rechristened the SOUTHLAND. The "new" train carried lightweight coaches, a coach-buffet-lounge and a reinstated 14-4 sleeper, all of which terminated at Birmingham. Frisco exited the passenger business altogether on December 8, 1967. By this time, the SOUTHLAND had once again lost the sleeper, and was the only varnish left in Frisco's once-extensive timetable.

Nameless Trains 7-8 continued in service on the Southern, however. The 10-2 Atlanta-Brunswick sleeper hung on until December 1965, making it the last heavyweight Pullman in regular service anywhere in the United States. By this time, the trains were losing more than $20,000 a month and likely would have faced little trouble obtaining approval for discontinuance. However, to help ensure there would be no opposition from regulatory agencies, the train's Birmingham-Atlanta mail and express cars were transferred to the SOUTHERNER, thereby worsening even further the train's financial condition. Finally, coach-only Trains 7-8 were posted for discontinuance on December 9, 1966, and rolled into history after the requisite 30-day notice expired.

THE BROSNAN-CLAYTOR ERA

With or without Trains 7-8, however, by the mid-1960s Southern's passenger business was sinking fast. As noted previously, in 1945, Southern had taken in $74 million in passenger revenue. By 1955, that number had dwindled to a little more than $18 million, and by 1967, passenger revenues were down to $6.3 million, a decline of more than 90%--more, if the figures were adjusted for inflation! In 1966, Southern reported passenger operating losses of $16.6 million under the "ICC formula" then in use. (On a direct-cost basis, the trains were probably closer to breaking even.) By comparison, for that same year, the Pennsylvania reported losses of $45 million, Santa Fe $31 million and Illinois Central $18.5 million. Partly, of course, the decline was a reflection of reduced train-miles, and with it the loss of mail and express business. But under any accounting system, the simple fact was, by 1967, the traveling public was simply choosing not to ride trains.

Beginning with the appointment of D. W. Brosnan as president of the railway in 1962, Southern adopted an increasingly aggressive attitude toward train-offs. At Brosnan's direction, Vice President-Law Graham Claytor (who would later be lionized for championing the 1970s era SOUTHERN CRESCENT) systematically began truncating or removing one train after another from SR's timetable. The methods used were common to the period: Sever connections at important endpoints, eliminate sleeping and/or dining car service, create inconvenient schedules, and when people stopped riding, claim huge operating losses and appeal to state and federal regulatory agencies for relief. Southern, however, employed an additional, innovative approach. Under federal law, an interstate passenger train could be discontinued at a state border if its only stop on the other side of the border was its terminus. Further, if a train made only a single stop within a state, it was also free of the jurisdiction of state regulators. This created some interesting opportunities. Take, for instance, the case of the PONCE DE LEON.

Thought not a streamliner, in 1955 the Cincinnati-Jacksonville PONCE DE LEON was a reasonably well-patronized train. It handled coaches between Cincinnati and Jacksonville as well as sleepers between Detroit-Jacksonville and Cleveland-Tampa as well as a Detroit-Jacksonville restaurant-lounge-sleeper. The train also served as the Cincinnati connection for the CAROLINA SPECIAL, which split off at Oakdale, Tennessee for Asheville and Columbia, South Carolina. By the 1960s, however, the Cincinnati-Florida market had declined to the point that Nos. 1-2 were coach only, and losing money. How to get rid of it?

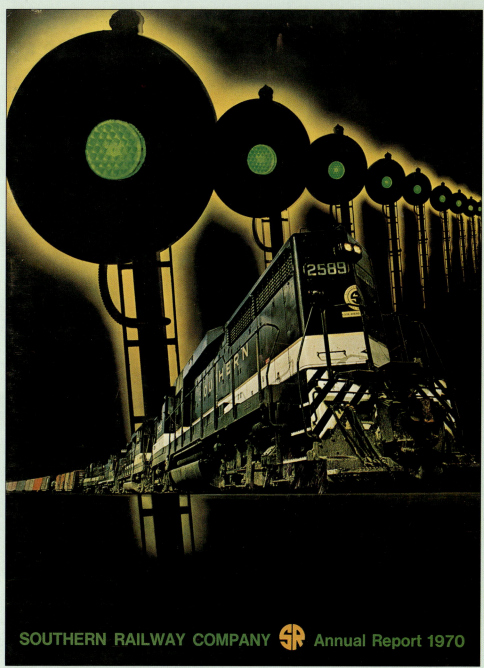

ABOVE • *Southern's 1970 Annual Report spoke with pride of the SOUTHERN CRESCENT, but also spoke frankly with stockholders about "increasingly unprofitable" passenger operations.*

One way would be to take on the ICC or the state regulatory agencies directly, an iffy proposition that often created considerable ill-will among the public and state and local governments. The other option was to create a case so airtight that no effective opposition was likely to arise. In 1963 Southern chose the second path with the PONCE DE LEON. It did this by changing without advance notice the train's southern terminus from Jacksonville to Council, Georgia, a kink in the tracks just north of the Florida state line and the last stop before the train's southern terminus at Jacksonville. Following the change, ridership naturally plummeted and losses mounted as passengers could no longer make Florida connections. (In this instance, however, the move only partially paid off. Although the train was eventually cut back to Cincinnati-Atlanta, the railroad was not able to eliminate it altogether until December 1968.)

The case of the Charlotte-Augusta AUGUSTA SPECIAL was disposed of in similar fashion. Trains 31-32 operated between Charlotte and Augusta, in effect serving as the Augusta section of Trains 37-38, THE CRESCENT. In the summer of 1965, the SPECIAL was handling a Washington-Augusta coach and a Washington-Columbia sleeper on a leisurely 30 mph carding. In the summer of 1966, with losses mounting, the railroad went to work getting rid of the train. To do this, on October 16, 1966, the SPECIAL's end points of Charlotte and Augusta were abruptly (and legally) eliminated, as they were the only stops within North Carolina and Georgia. This left the train operating entirely within South Carolina, running between Fort Mill in the north and Warrenville in the south. As the move was made without prior notification, passengers on the final "through" run were bused the last 12 miles between Warrenville and Augusta, and the mail was forwarded in trucks. With little patronage as a nowhere-to-nowhere run entirely within the state of South Carolina, the train was eliminated without opposition a few months later.

From the standpoint of the railroad, this hard-nosed approach paid off. By early 1971, when most railroads were preparing to hand over whatever was left of their passenger trains to Amtrak, Southern had reduced its own service, and its operating losses, to a point that it could afford to continue on its own. As of May 1, 1971, the only trains left in Southern's timetable were Nos. 1-2, the Washington-Atlanta SOUTHERN CRESCENT (with three day a week service between Atlanta and New Orleans); Nos. 5-6, the Washington-Atlanta PIEDMONT, with a tri-weekly Salisbury-Asheville connection that came to be known as the ASHEVILLE SPECIAL; and nameless Nos. 17-18 (later renumbered 7-8), the remnant of the Washington-Birmingham BIRMINGHAM SPECIAL, now operating between Washington and Lynchburg, with continuing service to Bristol via the Norfolk & Western. Amtrak elected not to retain N&W's leg of the operation, reducing the train to its final Washington-Lynchburg routing.

For various reasons, six railroads eventually elected not to join Amtrak. These were Rock Island, Rio Grande, Chicago, South Shore & South Bend, Georgia, Reading and, of course, Southern. Interestingly, Southern's wholly-owned subsidiary Central of Georgia did join, eliminating in the process the Atlanta-Savannah NANCY HANKS II and the Birmingham-Albany, Georgia leg of Illinois Central's every-other-day CITY OF MIAMI. According to then-president Graham Claytor, Southern made its decision based not on financial considerations (it would have cost $9.8 million to join--costly, but affordable), but on management's desire to retain control of its own operations and of the quality of service of the trains. In plain terms, SR did not want bad trains run badly on its busy Washington-Atlanta main line. In a 1974 interview, Claytor was somewhat more direct: "We made the decision [not to join] because we could afford to."

Ultimately, Southern did join Amtrak, but not before the SOUTHERN CRESCENT had gained considerable acclaim as the best passenger train in the country. Throughout the 1970s, the SOUTHERN CRESCENT seemed to be everything Amtrak was not. The train was clean. It ran on good track. It ran on time, with equipment that functioned properly. It served real meals in a real dining car and served them on real china with real silverware. It was classy. It had the visible support of railroad management, including Claytor himself. And it made friends everywhere it went.

During the 1975 and 1976, Southern was able to rid itself of its other three remaining train pairs. Under the terms of the Amtrak enabling legislation, nonparticipating railroads were required to operate their passenger trains

THE BICENTENNIAL STORY OF SOUTHERN RAILWAY

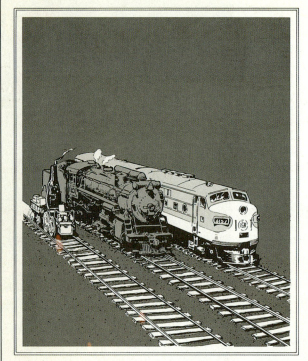

OUT OF THE PAST AND INTO THE FUTURE

ABOVE • *In time for the nation's 200th birthday, in 1976 SR produced "The Bicentennial Story of Southern Railway.*

until at least January 1, 1975. After that, they were once again free to request permission to drop them. Once eligible, Southern wasted no time pruning its deadwood. Trains 7-8, the one-car Lynchburg-Washington job that ran as part of a piggyback train for most of its route tied up for the last time that same year. Trains 3-4, the two-car ASHEVILLE SPECIAL, which had become a real tourist favorite thanks to the regular assignment of an ex-Wabash dome coach, made its last run on August 8, 1975. Trains 5-6, the PIEDMONT, died in November 1976. By then, it was running on a daylight schedule between Washington-Charlotte and was operating basically as a long-distance mixed train. That left the SOUTHERN CRESCENT, period. Though no application was made in 1975 for its outright discontinuance, the railroad did request, and was granted authorization, to trim the portion of the run between Atlanta and Birmingham from daily to three times a week.

Time finally ran out for the venerated flagship in 1979, though not without a struggle. In the summer of 1978, Southern applied to the ICC requesting permission to drop the train. In its brief, the railroad cited annual 1977 operating losses of $6.7 million and ridership that had declined to 165,000, or about 225 passengers per train per day. In addition, although the train was still well-maintained, much of its equipment was 30 or more years old, and it was simply and finally wearing out. Even a company with pockets as deep as Southern's could not justify investing in new passenger cars and diesels to re-equip a train that was consuming two dollars in costs for every dollar of revenue.

In all, 21 hearings were held in on-line communities, and although the ICC's law judge recommended in favor of the railroad, the ICC by a 4-3 vote directed Southern to continue operating the train for another year, until August 4, 1979. The decision was based, in large part, upon the company's overall good financial health, and, ironically, that the train continued to attract customers. This time, however, Southern had the public on its side. Wrote the *Birmingham News*: "The railroad has made a valiant effort, and its reward is to be stuck for another year keeping nostalgia alive." Added the *Greenville* (SC) *News*: "Greenville, as one of the stops on the route...would mourn the train's demise. Yet we can't expect a railroad company to spend millions of dollars to keep the past alive."

Failing in its attempt to eliminate the train outright, Southern then turned to Amtrak, which agreed on December 13, 1978, to take over operation of the CRESCENT, effective February 1, 1979. Under the terms of the contract, Southern would pay Amtrak $6,674,812, the amount the train had lost during its previous 12 months of operation, in eight monthly installments. A separate lease-purchase agreement was executed to cover the transfer of equipment required to protect the service. For its part, Amtrak agreed to continue operation of the "new" CRESCENT daily between Washington and Atlanta. A bonus for passengers was that the Atlanta-New Orleans part of the run, including the Los Angeles-New York transcontinental sleeper, would be increased from three times a week to daily. Amtrak also agreed to offer employment to the train's waiters, porters and cooks.

The last run of the SOUTHERN CRESCENT proved to be a gala, if bittersweet occasion. At Atlanta's Peachtree Station, television crews and a large crowd of well-wishers threatened to overwhelm the compact waiting room. Aboard the train, souvenir tickets "Commemorating 148 Years of Passenger Service" and depicting the "Best Friend of Charleston" locomotive side by side with a PS-4 Pacific and a modern passenger diesel were issued. Carrying the markers for the last No. 2 was business car No. 1, assigned for this trip to former SR President (and Secretary of the Navy) W. Graham Claytor and SR presidential assistant James A. Bistline, who had for many years been a mainstay of Southern's steam excursion program.

The next morning, as the last No. 1 rolled into Atlanta, it was time to bring the curtain down for the final time. On an adjacent track to meet the CRESCENT was the "Best Friend of Charleston" steam train. At trackside, Mr. Lou Sak, who had served for many years as Southern's General Manager for Passenger Sales and Service, removed a ceremonial Southern Railway flag from the front coupler of E8 no. 6909 and replaced it with an Amtrak flag, thus symbolizing the passing of the train from Southern to Amtrak control. Later, a luncheon was held at Atlanta's Diplomat Restaurant to honor a number of Southern employees who had helped make the SOUTHERN CRESCENT name synonymous with quality service. At the luncheon, Mr. Sak remarked: "Giving up the CRESCENT has been a heartbreaking thing for all of us. But we had to do this because the train was losing too much money." True enough, but perhaps the station announcer said it best the night before. As the last No. 2 pulled into Peachtree Station, the announcer said:

"Here comes the SOUTHERN CRESCENT, all the way from New Orleans. Thank you for riding Southern all these years."

ABOVE • *"Have a Nice Trip...Hurry Back!"* A well-dressed couple catches a breath of fresh air along the platform in Birmingham as Train No. 1, the SOUTHERN CRESCENT, lays over during its tri-weekly run between Atlanta and New Orleans. The scene of relative desolation in the background is evidence of the urban renewal program that claimed the original Terminal Station in late 1969. (J. W. Swanberg photo)

ABOVE • A sizable lashup of Southern and Central of Georgia road power moves slowly through Atlanta on its way to Pegram Shops on a sunny afternoon in January 1971. Along for the ride this day are RS-3 2039, delivered with a steam boiler for passenger service (removed during shopping in 1959), slug 2473 (rebuilt from an Alco RS1), a GE 45-ton switcher, C of G E8s 811 and 812 and three unidentified SR cab units. *(W. B. Folsom photo)*

LEFT • What kind of a passenger train is this? Actually, it's mail and express Train 21, seen here in January 1971 at the piggyback terminal in Alexandria, Virginia. Number 21 is powered by five (count 'em) F-units trailing a heavyweight rider coach, a couple of express-baggage cars and an apparently endless string of piggyback flats. This train does not appear in public timetables, meaning the general public is not invited to ride.
(Emery Gulash, Morning Sun Books Collection)

RIGHT • A face that is eminently familiar to long-time members of the railfan community is that of David P. Morgan, who served as editor of *Trains* magazine for four decades. A gifted writer and an unabashed steam fan (particularly if the locomotive in question was lettered Louisville & Nashville), Morgan here shares a quiet moment in Birmingham with Southern 2-8-0 722 during a fan trip in March 1971.
(Jim Thorington photo)

Left, Above • By the spring of 1971, time had all but run out on privately operated passenger trains in the United States, and, although Southern would prove an exception, subsidiary Central of Georgia would not. It was during this period that noted Midwest rail photographer George Strombeck set out to ride and record passenger trains as they once were. In April 1971, George journeyed to Savannah, Georgia to catch a ride on C of G Train 7, the NANCY HANKS II, seen here under the picturesque train shed at Savannah's historic depot.

(George Strombeck photo)

Left, Below • Despite the late date, the NANCY HANKS II still offered a remarkable array of amenities, including reclining seat lightweight coaches, a grill-lounge serving breakfast and lunch en route and a former Wabash dome coach that once ran on the joint (with Union Pacific) CITY OF ST. LOUIS. Here the NANCY pauses to board riders at Tennille, Georgia, near the midpoint of the day's run. *(George Strombeck photo)*

Above • The NANCY, following an on-time arrival at Spring Street Station in Atlanta. Number 7 was scheduled for a 1:00 PM arrival in Atlanta, which left plenty of time to turn and service the train in time for its 6:00 PM departure for the return trip to Savannah. Sadly, time ran out for the handsome little streamliner on May 1, 1971, as Nos. 7-8 did not survive into the Amtrak era. *(George Strombeck photo)*

Below • Once upon a time things were different and the Central of Georgia could hand out fancy match packs advertising its passenger service. *(Morning Sun Books Collection)*

Above • Seems like a lot of power for a one-car train, doesn't it? We're looking at Georgia Railroad Train 2, the daily local between Atlanta and Augusta, waiting for its 4:15 PM departure from Atlanta in April 1971. Two boiler-equipped GP7s, one from the Georgia road and one from sister Atlanta & West Point, are on the point this afternoon.

(George Strombeck photo)

Above • Well, now we know why two Geeps were necessary. Georgia No. 2 is a mixed train, and if that description conjures up a vision of a three-car freight trailed by a wooden combine, check this train out! Photographed from the vestibule of a former CRESCENT streamlined coach, the freight portion of the train stretches out of sight around a graceful curve on its way to Augusta. For reasons having to do with state taxes, the Georgia Railroad elected not to turn its trains over to Amtrak (though it seems unlikely this run would have survived the May 1, 1971 bloodletting), and thus continued to operate well into the 1970s.

(George Strombeck photo)

Above • One more look at the Georgia mixed, this time from inside the lone streamlined coach. In addition to photographer Strombeck, the entire ridership consisted of the train conductor and a deadheading crew member. There is no mention in the caption information of whether No. 2 was able to stick anywhere close to its scheduled 3-hour 45-minute running time, but either way, wouldn't this have been a fun train to ride? *(George Strombeck photo)*

Right • Early in the Amtrak era, the fledgling carrier was busy trying to convince the public their trains were "worth riding again." Southern, for its part, had an interest in demonstrating its willingness to cooperate with Amtrak in fitting into Amtrak's national transportation network. The result was this ad, which ran in late 1971 promoting Atlanta-Chicago rail service by way of Cincinnati. *(Author's collection)*

Above • The date of this photo is July 16, 1971, and that means Southern, in the company of the Georgia Road, the Rock Island, the Rio Grande, the South Shore and the Reading, stands apart in having taken a pass on membership in Amtrak, the government-funded agency that took over the nation's rail passenger service on May 1. Here a somewhat grubby gathering of Southern power share the ready tracks at Ivy City in Washington. Hold on to your hats, though, as a change is already in the wind, at least for Alabama Great Southern E8 6911. Shortly she will be reborn in a striking new green and white livery and be part of the power pool assigned to the premiere SOUTHERN CRESCENT.

(Collection of Gib Allbach)

Above • At its peak, Southern's fleet of Alco RS3 units reached 148. Of these, 47 were delivered with steam generators for at least occasional passenger service, including no. 2033, seen here operating on the point of the "Branchville Special," a NRHS movement that took place in the summer of 1971. Interestingly, 2033 is flying somewhat under false pretenses as a passenger locomotive, as its steam generator was removed during a shopping in 1961. No matter, though. On this sunny South Carolina afternoon, it's doubtful if there's much need for steam heat back in the coaches. *(Doug Nuckles photo)*

Above • It's tempting to title this photo something like "The past meets the future," but that's not quite the way things worked out. In the late 1960s, United Aircraft attempted to develop a solution to the problem of decreasing patronage aboard the nation's passenger trains. The result was the futuristic-looking Turbo Train, seen here adjacent to the "old-fashioned" SOUTHERN CRESCENT in Birmingham in the summer of 1971. Powered by an aircraft-type turbine, Turbo Train made an extensive barnstorming tour around the country before settling into scheduled Amtrak service over the former New Haven main line through Connecticut and Rhode Island. Sadly, the Turbos were troublesome in the extreme and were out of service for good within a relatively few years, although they were able to last a while longer in Canada.

(Jim Thorington photo)

Above • End of the line. In 1939, St. Louis Car Company and Fairbanks-Morse teamed up to build four motor trains, including the CRACKER, the VULCAN, the GOLDENROD and the JOE WHEELER for short haul service on the Southern. The little trains (one power car, one trailer coach) performed yeoman service into the 1950s, when two of the power cars were sold to short lines Georgia Northern and Georgia & Florida. In this view, taken at Moultrie, Georgia in March 1972, Georgia Northern Number 2, contemplates a future that extends no further than an impending date with the scrapper's torch.

(Collection of Gib Allbach)

Left • Fairbanks-Morse 1939 ad.

(Morning Sun Books Collection)

Below • The angle chosen by the photographer seems entirely fitting as it captures the proud face of E8 6907 at Ivy City in May 1972. The unit has recently received its new green, white and gold livery, including a Southern emblem on the nose and the SOUTHERN CRESCENT train name emblazoned on its cheeks. In 1972, given the state of passenger railroading elsewhere, did any other group of locomotives look sharper? *(George Berisso photo)*

A fair number of folks are on hand to help send SOUTHERN CRESCENT No. 2 on her way to Atlanta on this sunny May 27, 1972. Three E8s are obviously too much power for the four-car consist, but the train will pick up a dining car, two additional sleepers and at least two more coaches in Atlanta before departing for the overnight dash to Washington, New York and Boston. *(George Berisso photo)*

ABOVE • FP7 6133 is in charge of the ASHEVILLE SPECIAL at its namesake city in the summer of 1972. Trains 3-4, the SPECIAL, was a tri-weekly operation, running Sundays, Tuesdays and Fridays between Asheville and Salisbury, North Carolina, where it connected with Trains 5-6, the PIEDMONT to and from Washington. That dome coach bringing up the markers this afternoon is number 1613, *nee* Wabash 203. Following the end of Southern passenger service, the car was shipped north to Canada's Quebec, North Shore & Labrador. *(Collection of Gib Allbach)*

BELOW • Rather grubby power for Washington-Atlanta Train 5, the PIEDMONT, rumbles beneath Pennsy wire at Washington in this stunning telephoto shot. Obviously the care Southern lavished on the CRESCENT (and to some extent the ASHEVILLE SPECIAL) did not extend to this former maid of all work. Apart from coaches, the only onboard amenity offered was snack bar service between Washington and Charlotte.

(Emery Gulash, Morning Sun Books Collection)

Above • We're on the road with George Strombeck again, this time at Danville, Virginia. Danville is 235.8 timetable miles south of Washington Union Station and was a refueling stop for Southern No. 5, the PIEDMONT, on her daylight run to Atlanta. If No. 6 is on time, the north- and southbound sections of the PIEDMONTS will meet near Reidsville, North Carolina, a little more than 20 miles further down the line. In the meantime, No. 5's four FPs slake their considerable thirst during the scheduled 10-minute station stop.
(George Strombeck photo)

Left • Another look at the PIEDMONT at Danville. Car 951 is a coach-lounge delivered by the Budd Company in late 1949 for the general service pool. She'll be in the consist providing snack and beverage service as far as Charlotte. There, the car will be serviced and returned back north in the consist of tomorrow's Train 6.
(George Strombeck photo)

BELOW • Railfans familiar with George Strombeck's photographic work know that one of his specialties is night photography. Here, we're at Salisbury, North Carolina awaiting the arrival of Train 2, the northbound SOUTHERN CRESCENT. You have to be dedicated to stick around for this arrival, as she's not due until 1:06 AM. *(George Strombeck photo)*

RIGHT • According to the caption information provided on the slide, No. 2 is on time as she rolls into Salisbury just after 1:00 AM in August 1972. From here, it'll be a little over seven hours until her scheduled arrival in Washington at 8:15 AM. Through cars continue beyond DC to New York and Boston, including a Boston-Los Angeles 10-6 sleeper that continues a tradition of coast to coast sleeping car service that originated as a New York-Los Angeles car running over the Southern Pacific, Southern and Penn Central.

(George Strombeck photo)

ABOVE • When Southern elected not to participate in Amtrak, it was obligated to operate its remaining four pairs of passenger trains at least until 1975. In the case of the SOUTHERN CRESCENT and the ASHEVILLE SPECIAL, the trains ran with style. With the PIEDMONT and Trains 7-8, the Lynchburg-Washington remains of the old BIRMINGHAM SPECIAL, the case was somewhat different, as these rather quickly devolved into little more than long-distance mixed trains. Seen here getting ready to depart Lynchburg, No. 7 is headed by a string of GP30s and a single F-unit ahead of its lone coach and the "real" train, a solid consist of 30 or more piggyback flats.

(George Strombeck photo)

LEFT • Number 7 takes on fuel at Charlottesville before continuing north. Note the single heavyweight coach buried back behind the Geeps.

(George Strombeck photo)

Left • Dinner in the diner aboard No. 7, as an entrepreneuring "butch" serves up coffee and snacks during the layover at Charlottesville. According to one railfan familiar with the operation, he turned on the air conditioner when bringing around the hot food and fired up the heat when serving cold sandwiches and soft drinks. Now, that's enterprise for you! *(George Strombeck photo)*

Right • This is the train that finally showed up at Washington. Gone are the freight power and the TOFC cars, left behind at Alexandria. What's left is the coach and the single FP7. A far cry from elegance then and now, but a fascinating memory in today's era of Amtrak homogeneity. *(George Strombeck photo)*

Below • Budd-built Burlington dome coach lettered for Northern Pacific's NORTH COAST LIMITED is the feature car in this day's SOUTHERN CRESCENT seen here at Birmingham in September 1972. A couple of cars back is what appears to be a Southern Pacific dining car. *(Jim Thorington photo)*

Left • Quite a ways off our Southern "patch," but noteworthy nevertheless. Southern Mikado 4501 frequently found itself used in off-line excursion service, drawing a crowd wherever it went. On June 29, 1973 the venerable Mike makes an appearance in Wisconsin, heading up the annual Schlitz Brewing Company Old Milwaukee Special (Old Milwaukee is a brand of beer especially familiar to college students on a tight budget), which ran every summer from Baraboo to Milwaukee.

(Emery Gulash, Morning Sun Books Collection)

ABOVE • The SOUTHERN CRESCENT awaits its departure time at what remains of the passenger terminal in Birmingham, Alabama in July 1973. The bulk of the train's business had always been between Washington and Atlanta, as evidenced by the two E8s and abbreviated consist that is all but obscured by the supports for the umbrella sheds. *(Morning Sun Books Collection)*

RIGHT • For those who have never had the chance to ride one, here's the view from aboard dome-parlor 1602 as it rolls through the countryside between Birmingham and Atlanta in the consist of SOUTHERN CRESCENT No. 2. The car was originally built in August 1952 for the Wabash as a 21-seat parlor, 11-seat drawing room car for the Chicago-St. Louis BLUEBIRD. In its original configuration it was sold to the Central of Georgia in 1969, thence to Southern in 1970, where it operated in CRESCENT service between New Orleans and Atlanta.
(George Strombeck photo)

RIGHT • In the days prior to the formation of Amtrak, Southern frequently used the PEACH QUEEN as a means of ferrying motive power to and from Atlanta's Pegram shops. However, No. 29 did not survive into the Amtrak era. So it was that in later years, the job was picked up by Nos. 5-6, the PIEDMONT, seen here at Greenville, South Carolina in August 1973 with a pair of Alco road switchers cut in ahead of No. 6's regular FP7 power.

(George Strombeck photo)

ABOVE • In an effort to maximize train-miles, Southern frequently attached piggyback flats or other freight cars to the rear of its secondary passenger trains. Here a short cut of TOFC cars and a single auto rack bring up the markers (note the red flag stuck in the coupler) of PIEDMONT No. 6 as it departs Salisbury, North Carolina in the summer of 1973. Elegant, it's not, but it's an even money bet that most of the paying customers never even notice the flats at the rear of their train. The cars, by the way, are Ford Torinos.

(George Strombeck photo)

ABOVE • There's something magical about a railroad at night, wouldn't you agree? In August 1973, ASHEVILLE SPECIAL No. 3 arrives in its namesake town behind GP7 8275 and its regularly assigned FP7. The cab unit must have experienced a breakdown en route, as the combined 3,000 horsepower of the two units is far more than required by the train's two-car consist. *(George Strombeck photo)*

ABOVE • Although Southern certainly had the resources to operate it in better style, the company apparently figured one first-rate train was sufficient to maintain public relations, As a result, as time passed, Nos. 5-6, the PIEDMONT began to take on an increasingly dog-eared appearance. Witness this day's consist at Salisbury in August 1973: Four FP7s, a string of heavyweight express cars (plus one deadhead heavywright coach), a couple of rider coaches and a half-dozen or so TOFC cars. Not exactly up to the standard of the CRESCENT. *(Collection of Gib Allbach)*

ABOVE • Striking a pose reminiscent of publicity photos dating from the streamliner era, green-and-white Southern E8s 6916 and 6907 catch a little sunshine in the company of a somewhat more garishly hued Amtrak E8 251. In case you're wondering, 251 was built in 1952 as Seaboard Air Line Railroad 3055. Following the merger with Atlantic Coast Line, it reemerged as SCL 594 before being sold to the fledgling national passenger carrier in 1971. *(Gordon Lloyd photo)*

Above • An early proponent of diesel locomotive power, Southern had completely dropped its fires by 1953, due in part to the acquisition of a sizable fleet of EMD FTs. As these groundbreaking units reached the end of their service lives, most were either scrapped or returned to EMD as trade-ins for new units. In a few cases, however, the FTBs found new life on the Southern, as witness heater cars 960601and 960602, seen here at Atlanta on August 17, 1973. *(Collection of Gib Allbach)*

Above • Well, this is about as basic as you can get. Spanking-clean Washington-Lynchburg Train 7 clatters out of Alexandria, Virginia on a sunny afternoon in October 1973. Not much to look at now, but just wait! Immediately ahead is SR's intermodal terminal, where the little train will pick up several additional road units and a lengthy cut of thirty or more TOFC cars. *(T. J. Donohue photo)*

Above • The SOUTHERN CRESCENT arrives in Atlanta on the first day of November, 1973 behind the usual complement of four E8s. Four days a week, the train, in reduced form, continued beyond Atlanta to New Orleans (daily to Birmingham). On those days, when the transcontinental sleeper ran, there was an overnight layover in the Big Easy before the car departed the following afternoon on Amtrak's SUNSET LIMITED. Passengers traveling beyond New Orleans were permitted to use the sleeper as their hotel after they enjoyed a night on the town.

(Collection of Matt Herson)

Right • Far as she goes. Nameless Train 7 arrives at Lynchburg looking very much the same as it did when it left Washington, but the look is deceiving. At Monroe, Virginia, seven miles up the line, the minuscule consist was separated from its freight power and TTX equipment that had made the operation a mixed train over most of its route. The TTX cars, meanwhile, continued to Atlanta as a "pure" intermodal train.
(Matt Herson photo)

Above • Hallmark of a "name" train in the early days of railroading was the brass-railed observation car, where first-class passengers could watch the miles roll by as they caught a breath of outside air. Update the idea by half a century and you have Southern Car 19, the *Buena Vista*. However, this car is not for the paying passengers, but is used as a track inspection car. Inside, there is theater-style seating for 28, a dining area that seats 18 as well as a kitchen and a crew dorm. To protect the huge expanse of glass when not in use, a screen is attached. The car is seen here in Birmingham in 1974. Aptly, the photographer calls this captivating shot "Reflections in Steel." *(Jim Thorington photo)*

Left • Looking as though a few days have gone by since its last pass through the wash rack, E8 6907 enjoys the late winter sunshine outside Pegram Shops in Atlanta. The career of this unit continued beyond her days as power for the SOUTHERN CRESCENT, as she was sold to the New Jersey DOT in 1979 and renumbered 4331.
(W. B. Folsom photo)

ABOVE • Although the stunning green E8s got most of the attention, Southern also retained a fleet of 20 FP7 units, including nos. 6130-6149, for service on its remaining secondary passenger runs. Although the FP7s were not repainted green for regular service, they were nevertheless mechanically (thought not always cosmetically) well-maintained throughout their remaining service lives. Here CNO&TP 6136 idles beneath the sanding tower at Asheville, North Carolina, two days after Christmas in 1974. *(Collection of Gib Allbach)*

ABOVE • We're at 22nd Street crossing in Birmingham checking out the arrival of the SOUTHERN CRESCENT. From Birmingham, the train will head southwestward for the remainder of its daylight run to New Orleans. Beyond Atlanta, the consist is slim, including only Washington and Boston coaches, an Atlanta-New Orleans dining car and the transcontinental sleeper.

(Emery Gulash, Morning Sun Books Collection)

Right • Southern's decision to keep its passenger trains after May 1, 1971 probably did not make sense from a strictly financial standpoint. Although the company avoided paying a roughly $9.8 million "entrance fee," it unquestionably incurred operating losses far in excess of what it saved. What SR *did* get was publicity, all favorable, as it ran its premiere train in the grand style of the 1950s streamliner era. To help ensure its trains looked as good on the road as they did in print, the company seized on the opportunity to upgrade its image, including new paint for its E8 locomotives that featured the train name painted in gold just below the number boards. In February 1975, E8 6912 shows off her style during a layover at Birmingham. *(Emery Gulash, Morning Sun Books Collection)*

Above • Although the remainder of Southern's passenger fleet did not get the green-and-white treatment for its locomotives, travel accounts from the period indicate that the railroad ran its secondary trains professionally and staffed them with courteous crews. Be that as it may, no time was lost seeking regulatory approval to remove the trains once the mandatory period for operating them expired. Already on borrowed time, the four car (plus piggyback) Piedmont pays a call at Lynchburg in May 1975. In a little less than eighteen months, she'll tie up for the last time.
(Emery Gulash, Morning Sun Books Collection)

Left • Can't you almost smell the honeysuckle? The depot as Asheville, North Carolina presents a welcoming image in this view dating from the summer of 1975. At this point, the Asheville Special is less than three months from making her last run. *(George Strombeck photo)*

RIGHT • An unusual view of dome coach 1613 during its layover at Asheville shows the detail of the riveted roof and roof walk. Following Wabash-Nickel Plate-Norfolk & Western merger, the car was renumbered 1613 and re-lettered for the N&W while retaining its yellow and gray livery. In 1970, the car was sold to the Central of Georgia and passed into the hands of the Southern the following year.
(George Strombeck photo)

BELOW • A big part of the ASHEVILLE SPECIAL's customer base was school groups, due in large part to its uncommonly pretty scenery and friendly onboard crews. Just such a group of youngsters board No. 4 at Asheville on a sparkling day in June 1975. This is perhaps one of the last boardings of its kind, as the little trains made their final runs on August 8 of that year. Just for the fun of it, why don't we go along for the ride? *(George Strombeck photo)*

LEFT • Most of the kids seem to be captivated by the scenery, but at least a couple appear to be checking out the photographer to see what he's up to! We're inside dome-coach 1613 as it rolls out of Asheville. One thing seems sure, however, and that is that Southern kept the car in good maintenance right up until the end of operations. Notice, there are still headrests on the seat backs, curtains in the windows and etched glass in the bulkhead mirrors.
(George Strombeck photo)

BELOW • One look out of the vestibule door tells you what was the biggest selling feature of the ASHEVILLE SPECIAL. The scenery is simply splendid as Train 4 rolls east toward Salisbury. In the consist this day are *Fort Mitchell*, a baggage-coach originally built In 1947 for the Central of Georgia, a 660-series coach (also built in 1947 for Central's NANCY HANKS II) and dome-coach 1613. *(George Strombeck photo)*

Right • We're inside the waiting room at Southern's depot in Salisbury, North Carolina, eastern terminus for the Asheville Special, waiting for the arrival of Train 6, the connecting Piedmont. Indicative of the company's spit-and-polish approach to most things passenger related, the depot is clean and well-maintained. Amidst the air of general good order at Salisbury is an ominous note in the form of a discontinuance notice posted for Nos. 3-4, the Asheville Special. The end wasn't long in coming, either. The little trains made their last runs on August 8, 1975, just a few months after this photo was made.
(George Strombeck photo)

Above • If both trains are on time, the eastbound Asheville Special arrived in Salisbury at 1:15 PM in anticipation of a meet with the northbound Piedmont, scheduled in at 2:20 PM. In this photo from the summer of 1975, both trains appear to be close enough to on time to permit across-the-platform connections for passengers off the Special bound for Greensboro, Lynchburg, Charlottesville or Washington. It looks like there's plenty of power heading up today's No. 6, including freight GP18 190. *(George Strombeck photo)*

Left • An uncommonly lengthy Southern Crescent awaits her departure time at New Orleans Union Passenger Terminal in November 1975. Once, there would have been trains from the Illinois Central, Southern Pacific, Missouri Pacific/Texas & Pacific, Louisville & Nashville and Kansas City Southern sharing the bumping posts with No. 2, but by this date, the only other trains calling at NOUPT are Amtrak's Sunset Limited and City of New Orleans. The terminal survives as a combined Amtrak-intercity bus terminal.
(J. W. Swanberg photo)

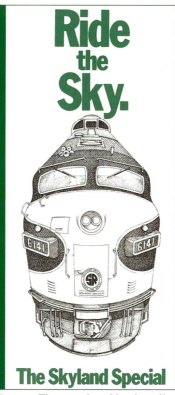

ABOVE • What train is this? Following the demise of the ASHEVILLE SPECIAL, Southern operated a purely tourist train called the SKYLAND SPECIAL, which ran on summer weekends between Asheville and Old Fort, North Carolina. Included in the train's consist were coaches, the ex-Wabash dome-parlor (called a "Bubble Car" in promotional literature) and open gondolas, which were probably empty given the downpour on this June 1976 day. Here it is on its return trip at High Fill, North Carolina, behind FP7 6133. The "open" gondolas actually had rudimentary roof covers on them. The 3-1/2 hour round trip cost six bucks and served up enough scenery to make it worth the price ten times over.

(Collection of Gib Allbach)

ABOVE • Flyer produced by the railroad promoting the SKYLAND SPECIAL: "A Ride in the Sky." The train operated the summer following the discontinuance of regular service into Asheville.

ABOVE • A final look at the PIEDMONT as it rolls through some uncommonly pretty fall scenery in early November 1976. By this time, the train had been cut back to a daylight schedule between Washington and Charlotte, usually running with a hefty cut of freight equipment. Southern received permission to discontinue the run, effective November 24, but as an accommodation to its customers during the holiday travel period, operated a "Thanksgiving Special" through the following weekend. With the passing of Nos. 5-6, the SOUTHERN CRESCENT remained as the last varnish anywhere on the system.

(Collection of Morning Sun Books)

Train Time In Atlanta

In the spring of 1977, the author had occasion to be in Atlanta on a business trip, and naturally took the first opportunity to venture out to Peachtree Street Station to catch a first look at Southern's pride and joy, the SOUTHERN CRESCENT, as it prepared to depart for its overnight run to Washington. At the time, the author was unfamiliar with the CRESCENT's operation, and so did not note whether this day's train was a through trip. However, the fact that there was a change of motive power during the train's dwell time indicates that the train did not originate in Atlanta. *(All photos by Greg Stout)*

RIGHT • The station building at Peachtree presented a neat (and surprisingly contemporary) appearance. At this point, it is still well before train time, and this evening's crowd has not yet begun to gather.

ABOVE • As the tracks are below street level (and hence, beneath the level of the waiting room), passengers are required to descend a long flight of stairs to reach the platform. Enjoying a momentary respite before boarding time, the baggage man enjoys a breath of fresh evening air with the engine crew.

ABOVE • The conductor and the brakeman descend the stairs to take charge of the train. This photo also shows clearly the complex arrangement of air tanks and piping on the roof of E8 6910.

ABOVE • First call for boarding! Passengers gather in the compact midway area between the waiting room and the stairs leading down to the platform.

RIGHT • Coaches to the front, sleepers to the rear. I did not make a detailed count, but as memory serves, there were upwards of 100 paying customers boarding this evening. The switch engine visible in the background has the road engines that arrived with the train in tow and is headed back to Pegram Shops. From this angle, the train's 10-car consist can clearly be seen above the roof of the umbrella shed.

BELOW • We're pretty well set to go as the locomotive crew boards the lead locomotive. Southern took extraordinarily good care of this train, as even the roofs of the engines appear to have been freshly scrubbed.

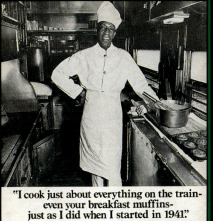

LEFT • In 1976 and 1977, Southern ran a series of ads promoting travel aboard the SOUTHERN CRESCENT, including this one featuring dining car chef Louis Price. Sadly, Price was among those killed on December 3, 1978, when northbound CRESCENT No. 2 derailed on a curve near Charlottesville, Virginia. NTSB investigators estimated the train entered the 45 MPH curve in excess of 80. Price had worked for the railroad since 1941.

(Author's collection)

BELOW • We're outta here, and on time no less, as nine thousand horsepower worth of E8's clear their throats after resting at idle for the past half hour. The next stop will be Gainesville, forty-nine miles and fifty-five minutes up the line.

119

Left, Above • Ex-Southern Pacific GS-4 4449, still wearing the livery applied for its role as power for the AMERICAN FREEDOM TRAIN, clatters across the diamond at 22nd Street in Birmingham on what the photographer characterizes as a "dreary morning" in the spring of 1977. Today's consist does not appear to be that of the FREEDOM TRAIN, but rather an excursion trip (note the presence of two dome coaches).
(Jim Thorington photo)

Left, Below • Railway Post Office cars and long strings of Railway Express equipment have been a thing of the past for more than a decade by the time this photo was taken at Birmingham in April 1978. However, it appears the SOUTHERN CRESCENT still handles at least a little bit of express business, though not nearly enough to absorb the increasing tide of red ink that will swallow up the train before another year has passed. *(David Hurt photo)*

Above • The SOUTHERN CRESCENT makes a fine sight as she pauses for a station stop at Danville, Virginia in May 1978. Night shots such as this were a specialty of photographer George Strombeck, who has managed to infuse this image with an atmosphere of mystery and romance reminiscent of Agatha Christie's *Murder on the Orient Express*. Fortunately, however, the caption information included with this slide makes no mention of any untimely deaths during the overnight run to Atlanta.
(George Strombeck photo)

Left • Even in the last year of operating the SOUTHERN CRESCENT, Southern was conscious of its image. *(Author's collection)*

Above • Breakfast time aboard No. 2 in May 1978, and if the crowd is any indication, the diner is turning a brisk business. (Sadly, after the railroad posted the train for discontinuance in the summer of 1978, "souvenir hunters" began to pilfer silverware at an alarming rate. By the time SR was able to secure its remaining sterling, there was barely enough left to assemble a single four-place setting.) SOUTHERN CRESCENT dining cars operated daily between Washington and Atlanta and between Atlanta and New Orleans on days the train ran through. For those more inclined toward liquid refreshment, there was also a tavern-lounge that operated Washington-Atlanta. *(George Strombeck photo)*

Right • The car identification number in the window, 110, indicates that this is a 52-seat coach southbound between Washington and New Orleans, and the timetable tells us that this car operates on Mondays, Wednesdays and Saturdays. On the return trip, car 210 runs Monday, Wednesday and Friday. *(George Strombeck photo)*

LEFT • During the Graham Claytor presidency, Southern made a consistent effort to maintain good public relations, among other ways, by keeping its flagship SOUTHERN CRESCENT in tip-top condition and sponsoring numerous steam excursions around the system. Not content to simply employ its own former motive power, SR also reached out to bring in other locomotives, such as former Texas & Pacific 2-10-4 610. In this photo, the big Texas-type is seen at Birmingham, heading north on its way to Chattanooga. From this angle, it's a mighty impressive sight!
(Jim Thorington photo)

BELOW • Despite the seemingly unlimited goodwill generated by the SOUTHERN CRESCENT, the railroad eventually had to face the fact that its equipment was simply wearing out, and even if the stockholders remained willing to turn a blind eye toward its operating losses, there was no financially prudent way to replace or upgrade its coaches and sleepers. Thus, in the summer of 1978, Southern petitioned for permission to discontinue operation of the train. In the last month of before Amtrak takeover, the CRESCENT is seen drumming along the main line west of Atlanta with three E8s up front and the dome coach bringing up the markers. *(Emery Gulash, Morning Sun Books Collection)*

ABOVE • After extensive negotiations, Southern and Amtrak agreed on February 1, 1979 as the date when the SOUTHERN CRESCENT would become the responsibility of the latter carrier. In this last photo of the train as a Southern operation, No. 2 crosses the causeway at Lake Ponchartrain, just outside New Orleans. In the consist this day are the transcontinental sleeper (seen wearing Amtrak red, white and blue, and dome-parlor 1602, which regularly ran in the consist between Atlanta and New Orleans. *(James B. Holder photo)*

BELOW • Following the turnover of the SOUTHERN CRESCENT, changes were not long in coming, as evidenced by this photo, taken at Irondale, Alabama in the summer of 1979. Already, there is Amtrak rolling stock in the consist and an Amtrak E9 (ex-UP 912) leading the way. Despite the inclusion of two Southern E8s on the point of this day's train, none of the green and white locomotives were ever transferred to Amtrak ownership. *(Jim Thorington photo)*

ABOVE • Amtrak's "New Look" CRESCENT rumbles into Birmingham behind F40 259 and an E8 in the "Phase Two" livery in March 1980. By this time, the train had been pretty much completely assimilated into Amtrak's operations, and it was difficult to find any remaining vestiges of the former Southern operation. *(Jim Thorington photo)*

RIGHT • Train board at Slidell, Louisiana, in March 1980. The departure times are slightly different from when the train was a Southern operation, and the timetable numbers have been changed to 19-20 (Amtrak's SUNSET LIMITED operate as 1-2). *(Collection of Morning Sun Books)*

BELOW • End of the trail. Along with Conrail 9947 and an unbelievably worn-out Penn Central E8, Southern 4249 sit forlornly in the yard at Elizabethport, New Jersey on September 7, 1980. *(J. W. Swanberg photo)*

APPENDIX A: SOUTHERN RAILWAY STREAMLINED PASSENGER CAR ROSTER

The following is a list of streamlined passenger cars owned by the Southern Railway, as well as selected cars acquired by carriers participating in through train service with Southern and cars acquired from the Central of Georgia following the merger. Cars purchased for dedicated service are listed together. Streamlined equipment purchased for the general passenger pool is listed according to car number by builder.

ST. LOUIS CAR COMPANY
MOTOR CAR AND TRAILER TRAINS

NUMBER	CAR TYPE	SERVICE DATE	NOTES
1	Power car	9/24/39	1
MT-1	Trailer coach	9/24/39	1
2	Power car	9/29/39	2
MT-2	Trailer coach	9/29/39	2
3, 4	Power car	10/11/39	3
MT-3, 4	Trailer coach	10/11/39	3
40, 41	Power car	8/24/39	4
MT-40, 41	Trailer coach	8/24/39	4

1. Operated at the Birmingham-Mobile GOLDENROD
2. Operated as the Oakdale-Tuscumbia JOE WHEELER
3. Operated as the Atlanta-Brunswick CRACKER
4. Operated as the Meridian-Chattanooga VULCAN

CARS BUILT FOR THE SOUTHERNER
Train placed in service March 31, 1941

NUMBER	CAR TYPE	BUILDER	CAR NAME	NOTES
700	22-seat coach-bagg.-dorm	P-S	Mississippi	1
701	22-seat coach-bagg.-dorm	P-S	District of Columbia	1
702	22-seat coach-bagg.-dorm	P-S	Delaware	1
900-902	52-seat divided coach	P-S	South Carolina	2, 7
800	56-seat coach	P-S	North Carolina	
801	56-seat coach	P-S	Maryland	
802-803	56-seat coach	P-S	Alabama	
804-805	56-seat coach	P-S	Georgia	
4030	56-seat coach	P-S	New York	3
4031	56-seat coach	P-S	New Jersey	3
4032	56-seat coach	P-S	Pennsylvania	3
3300-3302	48-seat dining car	P-S	Virginia	
1100-1102	Tavern-lounge-obs.	P-S	Louisiana	

1. Provided seating for colored passengers
2. Provided seating for 26 colored passengers and 26 white passengers
3. Cars 4030-4032 owned by the Pennsylvania Railroad

CARS BUILT FOR THE TENNESSEAN
Train placed in service May 18, 1941

NUMBER	CAR TYPE	BUILDER	CAR NAME	NOTES
1700	Baggage-mail-RPO	P-S	Corinth	
1701	Baggage-mail-RPO	P-S	Grand Junction	
1725	Baggage-mail-RPO	P-S	Lenoir City	
1726	Baggage-mail-RPO	P-S	Athens	
1750	Baggage-storage mail	P-S	Decatur	
1751	Baggage-storage mail	P-S	Greeneville	
703	22-seat coach-bagg.-dorm	P-S	Cleveland	1
704	22-seat coach-bagg.-dorm	P-S	Johnson City	1
705	22-seat coach-bagg.-dorm	P-S	Bedford	1
903	54-seat divided coach	P-S	Pulaski	2
904	54-seat divided coach	P-S	Loudon	2
905	54-seat divided coach	P-S	Morristown	2
806	6-seat coach	P-S	Huntsville	
807	56-seat coach	P-S	Buntyn	
808	56-seat coach	P-S	Sheffield	
809	56-seat coach	P-S	Radford	
810	56-seat coach	P-S	Bristol	
811	56-seat coach	P-S	Sweetwater	
812	56-seat coach	P-S	Charlottesville	
813	56-seat coach	P-S	Lynchburg	
814	56-seat coach	P-S	Roanoke	
3304	48-seat dining car	P-S	Chattanooga	
3304	48-seat dining car	P-S	Alexandria	
1150	Tavern-lounge-obs.	P-S	Washington	
1151	Tavern-lounge-obs.	P-S	Knoxville	
1152	Tavern-lounge-obs.	P-S	Memphis	
	12-1 Sleeper	Pullman	Brentwood	3
	12-1 Sleeper	Pullman	Dahlonega	3
	12-1 Sleeper	Pullman	Knickerbocker	3
	12-1 Sleeper	Pullman	Puritan	3
	10-3 Sleeper	Pullman	Villa Heights	3
	0-3 Sleeper	Pullman	Villa Nova	3
	10-3 Sleeper	Pullman	Villa Verde	3

1. Provided seating for colored passengers
2. Provided seating for colored and white passengers
3. Standard (heavyweight) sleepers painted to match streamlined consist

HEAD-END, COACH, LOUNGE AND DINING CARS BUILT FOR THE CRESCENT, SOUTHERNER and ROYAL PALM

CAR NUMBER	CAR TYPE	BUILDER	NAME	DATE	NOTES
87	Baggage-mail	P-S		1949	1
1120-1121	Baggage-mail	P-S		1949	2
1702-1703	Baggage-mail	P-S		1949	
710-711	Baggage-dorm	ACF		1950	
1598	Baggage-dorm	ACF		1950	2
1599	Baggage-dorm	P-S		1950	2
68-69	52-seat coach	Budd		1949	3
106	52-seat coach	Budd		1949	1
815-840	52-seat coach	Budd		1949	
3250-3251	52-seat coach	Budd		1949	2
	52-seat coach	Budd	Pahokee	1949	4
841-846	52-seat coach	P-S		1958	
3786-3789	52-seat coach	ACF		1950	
120	58-seat coach	Budd		1953	3
3252	58-seat coach	Budd		1949	2
501	48-seat diner	Budd		1949	3
2790	48-seat diner	Budd		1949	2
3305-3312	48-seat diner	Budd		1949	
3869	48-seat diner	Budd		1949	
950-955	Coach-lounge	Budd		1949	
3399, 3899	Diner-lounge	ACF		1950	
	Diner-lounge	ACF	South Bay	1950	4

Pullman-Standard Sleeping Cars Built for the Crescent and Royal Palm

CAR NUMBER	CAR TYPE	CAR NAME	DATE	NOTES
2300	5 DBR-lounge-obs	Royal Arch	1950	8, 10
2301	5 DBR-lounge-obs	Royal Court	1950	10
3499	5 DBR-lounge-obs	Royal Palm	1950	10
3300	5 DBR-lounge-obs	Royal Canal	1950	2
3301	5 DBR-lounge-obs	Royal Street	1950	2
	5 DBR-lounge-obs	Royal Palace	1950	1, 9
	5 DBR-lounge-obs	Royal Crest	1950	5
	5 DBR-lounge-obs	Azalea	1950	4
2350	1 MR-2 DR-lounge	Crescent City	1949	
2351	1 MR-2 DR-lounge	Crescent Harbor	1949	
2352	1 MR-2 DR-lounge	Crescent Moon	1949	
2353	1 MR-2 DR-lounge	Crescent Shores	1949	
2000	10-6 sleeper	Alapaha River	1949	
2001	10-6 sleeper	Altamaha River	1949	
2002	10-6 sleeper	Dan River	1949	
2003	10-6 sleeper	Catawba River	1949	
2004	10-6 sleeper	Enoree River	1949	
2005	10-6 sleeper	Flint River	1949	
2006	10-6 sleeper	Ocmulgee River	1949	
2007	10-6 sleeper	Otter River	1949	
2008	10-6 sleeper	Pacolet River	1949	
2009	10-6 sleeper	Potomac River	1949	
2010	10-6 sleeper	Rapidan River	1949	
2011	10-6 sleeper	Rivanna River	1949	
2012	10-6 sleeper	Saluda River	1949	
2013	10-6 sleeper	Seneca River	1949	
2014	10-6 sleeper	Shenandoah River	1949	
2015	10-6 sleeper	Rappahannock River	1949	
2016	10-6 sleeper	St. Johns River	1949	
2017	10-6 sleeper	Tiger River	1949	
2018	10-6 sleeper	Tombigbee River	1949	
2019	10-6 sleeper	Tugalo River	1949	
2020	10-6 sleeper	Tye River	1949	
2021	10-6 sleeper	Yadkin River	1949	
2022	10-6 sleeper	York River	1949	
2023	10-6 sleeper	Warrior River	1949	
3400	10-6 sleeper	Emory River	1949	
3400	10-6 sleeper	Mobile River	1949	2
3401	10-6 sleeper	French Broad River	1949	
3401	10-6 sleeper	Pearl River	1949	2
	10-6 sleeper	Chattahoochee River	1949	3
	10-6 sleeper	Alabama River	1949	1
	10-6 sleeper	Argentina	1949	4
	10-6 sleeper	Brazil	1949	4
	10-6 sleeper	Chile	1949	4
	10-6 sleeper	Guatemala	1949	4
	10-6 sleeper	Venezuela	1949	4
8351	10-6 sleeper	Birch River	1949	6
8352	10-6 sleeper	Bush River	1949	6
8353	10-6 sleeper	Delaware River	1949	6
8354	10-6 sleeper	Middle River	1949	6
8355	10-6 sleeper	Patapsco River	1949	6
8356	10-6 sleeper	Raritan River	1949	6
8357	10-6 sleeper	Schuylkill River	1949	6
8358	10-6 sleeper	Susquehanna River	1949	6

General Service Sleeping Cars built by Pullman-Standard

CAR NUMBER	CAR TYPE	CAR NAME	DATE	NOTES
2200	14-4 sleeper	Cashier's Valley	1949	
2201	14-4 sleeper	Hiwassee Valley	1949	
2202	14-4 sleeper	James River Valley	1949	
2203	14-4 sleeper	Mississippi Valley	1949	
2204	14-4 sleeper	Paint Rock Valley	1949	
2205	14-4 sleeper	Piedmont Valley	1949	
2206	14-4 sleeper	Roanoke Valley	1949	
2207	14-4 sleeper	Shenandoah Valley	1949	
2208	14-4 sleeper	Spring Valley	1949	
2209	14-4 sleeper	Tennessee Valley	1949	
2210	14-4 sleeper	Wauhatachie Valley	1949	

General Service Cars Acquired From Other Carriers

SOUTHERN NUMBER	CAR TYPE	BUILDER	CAR NAME	DATE BUILT	NOTES
660-663	56-seat coach	P-S		1947	11
664	56-seat coach	Budd	Fort Oglethorpe	1947	12
665	56-seat coach	Budd	Fort McPherson	1947	13
726	56-seat coach	ACF		1947	14
727	Coach-baggage	Budd	Fort Mitchell	1947	15
907	68-seat coach	ACF		1947	16
1602	Dome-parlor	P-S		1952	17
1613	36-seat dome coach	P-S		1958	18

Explanation of Notes:

1. Assigned to Western of Alabama
2. Owned by Louisville & Nashville
3. Assigned to Atlanta & West Point
4. Owned by Florida East Coast
5. Owned by New York Central
6. Owned by Pennsylvania Railroad
7. Converted to 22-seat coach-baggage-dormitory 706, 1952
8. Renamed *Luther Calvin Norris*, 1950
9. Renamed *Charles A. Wickersham*, 1952
10. Rebuilt as 11-double bedroom cars in 1958
11. Built as Central of Georgia 660-663 for Nancy Hanks II. Transferred to Southern 1971
12. Built as C of G 664. Transferred to Southern 1970
13. Built as C of G 665. Transferred to Southern 1970
14. Built as C of G 390. Renumbered 726 and transferred to Southern 1970
15. Built as C of G 391. Renumbered 727 and transferred to Southern 1970
16. Built as C of G "Jim Crow" coach 543. Renumbered 907 and transferred to Southern 1970
17. Built as Wabash 1602 for Blue Bird. Sold to C of G 1968. Transferred to SR 1971
18. Built as Wabash 203 for WAB-Union Pacific City of St. Louis. Sold to C of G 1970. Transferred to SR 1971

Pullman Car Types:
1 MR-2 DR-lounge ... 1 master room, 2 drawing room, buffet-lounge
5 DBR lounge-obs ... 5 double bedroom, buffet-lounge observation
12-1 ... 12 section, 1 drawing room
10-3 ... 10 section, 3 double bedroom
10-6 ... 10 roomette, 6 double bedroom
14-4 ... 4 roomette, 4 double bedroom

APPENDIX B: SOUTHERN RAILWAY PASSENGER DIESEL POWER ROSTER

The following lists all known Southern Railway (and affiliates) diesel-powered passenger locomotives, including units purchased for freight use and later fitted with steam generators, either for regular service or as protection power. Readers should note that this list is not all-inclusive in that non-steam generator-equipped units may have been used from time to time on scheduled passenger runs or special movements. Road number shown are original (as-delivered). Model designations are as-delivered and do not reflect rebuilds or upgrades.

ROAD NUMBER	BUILDER	MODEL	OWNER	DATE BUILT	DATE RETIRED
120, 122	EMD	GP7	CofG	1951	1981
121, 123	EMD	GP7	CofG	1951	1980
147	Alco	RS3	SR	1952	1974
148-150	Alco	RS3	SR	1953	1976
400-401	EMD	F2A	AE&C	1946	1961
801, 804, 806, 810	EMD	E7A	CofG	1946	1971
802, 805, 808, 809	EMD	E7A	CofG	1946	1970
803, 807	EMD	E7A	CofG	1946	1968
811-812	EMD	E8A	CofG	1950	1971
2025-2032	Alco	RS3	SR	1952	1976
2033	Alco	RS3	SR	1952	1974
2034	Alco	RS3	SR	1952	1976
2035	Alco	RS3	SR	1952	1974
2036	Alco	RS3	SR	1952	1972
2037	Alco	RS3	SR	1952	1976
2038	Alco	RS3	SR	1952	1974
2039	Alco	RS3	SR	1952	1976
2040	Alco	RS3	SR	1952	1972
2041-2044	Alco	RS3	SR	1952	1976
2045	Alco	RS3	SR	1952	1974
2046-2047	Alco	RS3	SR	1952	1976
2101-2105	Alco	RS2	SR	1949	1964
2106	Alco	RS2	SR	1949	1955
2107-2112	Alco	RS2	SR	1949	1964
2127-2130	Alco	RS2	SR	1949	1964
2156-2159	EMD	GP7	SR	1951	1981
2160-2161	EMD	GP7	SR	1951	1980
2162-2165	EMD	GP7	SR	1951	1981
2800-2802	EMD	E6A	SR	1941	1967
2900-2903	EMD	E6A	SR	1941	1967
2904	Alco	DL109	SR	1942	1954
2905-2908	EMD	E7A	SR	1948	1968
2909-2910	EMD	E7A	SR	1948	1967
2911-2915	EMD	E7A	SR	1948	1968
2916	EMD	E7A	SR	1948	1970
2917	EMD	E7A	SR	1948	1968
2918-2919	EMD	E7A	SR	1948	1970
2920-2922	EMD	E7A	SR	1948	1968
2923-2929	EMD	E8A	SR	1951	1979
4100B	EMD	FTB	SR	1943	1963
4101B	EMD	FTB	SR	1943	1958
4102B	EMD	FTB	SR	1943	1962
4100C	EMD	FTB	SR	1943	1958
4101C	EMD	FTB	SR	1943	1959
4102C	EMD	FTB	SR	1943	1961
4128	EMD	F3A	SR	1946	1963
4129	EMD	F3A	SR	1946	1972
4130	EMD	F3A	SR	1946	1972
4131	EMD	F3A	SR	1946	1963
4132	EMD	F3A	SR	1946	1955
4133-4141	EMD	F3A	SR	1946	1972
4142	EMD	F3A	SR	1946	1967
4143-4145	EMD	F3A	SR	1946	1972
4146	EMD	F3A	SR	1946	1967
4179	EMD	F3A	SR	1949	1967
4320-4327	EMD	F3B	SR	1946	1963
4329-4331	EMD	F3B	SR	1947	1963
4341-4346	EMD	F3B	SR	1947	1963
4347	EMD	F3B	SR	1947	1965
4348-4349	EMD	F3B	SR	1947	1963
4350	EMD	F3B	SR	1947	1965
4351	EMD	F3B	SR	1947	1965
4352	EMD	F3B	SR	1947	1963
6107	EMD	F3A	CNO&TP	1947	1969
6108	EMD	F3A	CNO&TP	1947	1961
6119	EMD	F7A	CNO&TP	1950	1973
6130-6134	EMD	FP7	CNO&TP	1950	1979
6135-6137	EMD	FP7	CNO&TP	1950	1979
6138	EMD	FP7	CNO&TP	1950	1988
6139-6140	EMD	FP7	CNO&TP	1950	1979
6141	EMD	FP7	CNO&TP	1950	1988
6142	EMD	FP7	CNO&TP	1950	1979
6143	EMD	FP7	CNO&TP	1950	1988
6144-6146	EMD	FP7	CNO&TP	1950	1979
6147	EMD	FP7	CNO&TP	1950	1988
6148-6149	EMD	FP7	CNO&TP	1950	1979
6169-6175	EMD	F7B	CNO&TP	1952	1969
6176	EMD	F7B	CNO&TP	1952	1967
6177-6183	EMD	F7B	CNO&TP	1952	1969
6200	EMD	GP7	CNO&TP	1950	1965
6201	EMD	GP7	CNO&TP	1950	1970
6202	EMD	GP7	CNO&TP	1950	1981
6203	EMD	GP7	CNO&TP	1950	1973
6204-6205	EMD	GP7	CNO&TP	1950	1981
6206-6207	Alco	RS2	CNO&TP	1949	1964
6400-6401	Alco	DL109	CNO&TP	1941	1954
6540	EMD	GP7	AGS	1950	1980
6541	EMD	GP7	AGS	1950	1981
6542	EMD	GP7	AGS	1950	1970
6543	EMD	GP7	AGS	1950	1981
6544	EMD	GP7	AGS	1950	1970
6700	EMD	F2A	AGS	1946	1963
6701	EMD	F2A	AGS	1946	1963
6702	EMD	F3A	AGS	1946	1972
6703	EMD	F3A	AGS	1946	1961
6704-6705	EMD	F3A	AGS	1946	1972
6706	EMD	F3A	AGS	1947	1973
6707-6708	EMD	F3A	AGS	1947	1973
6714-6715	EMD	F7A	AGS	1950	1973
6718-6719	EMD	F7A	AGS	1950	1973
6750-6751	EMD	F3B	AGS	1946	1963
6804	EMD	F3A	NO&NE	1947	1973
6805	EMD	F3A	NO&NE	1947	1963
6806	EMD	F3A	NO&NE	1947	1972
6900-6905	Alco	PA3	CNO&TP	1953	1965
6906	EMD	E8A	NO&NE	1951	1978
6907-6909	EMD	E8A	NO&NE	1951	1979
6910	EMD	E8A	NO&NE	1951	1978
6911-6915	EMD	E8A	NO&NE	1951	1979